S0-DTB-194

Dustin Hrycun

One Day I Was Swimming

A Vulnerably Honest Dialogue with Relationship

Aunt Sonia,
Page 93 is you.
Thank-you for always
being a source of
down-to-earth
wisdom.
-Dustin Hrycun

Copyright © 2011 Dustin Hrycun

All rights reserved.

ISBN-13: 978-1463633721
ISBN-10: 1463633726

To Coffee, Wine, and Beer, and the sanity you have provided.

Contents

1

Introduction

The summer I found myself was the exact same summer that I completely lost myself. One day I was swimming. I was in a wide-open lake, the cool refreshing water sliding across my bare skin, moving my arms and legs in a frog-like action. It was freeing. It was enlivening. It was a moment of peaceful solitude and independence where, and when, nothing and no one mattered. As I was fluidly turning myself around in the water a sudden pain struck my left hand. A quick glance down revealed an open wound in my palm. Treading water the best I could, I grabbed my left hand with my right uninjured one and began to examine my pain. Within the wound was what seemed to be a string-like wire. As I began to get my fingers on the agony-infesting wire in my hand, I came to realize that it was not a string-like wire but a real live worm working its way into my connection to touch and feel, burrowing deeper and deeper. Only a few short seconds passed before I noticed that the worm seemed much shorter and somewhat smaller than I had originally observed. The unfortunate reality was that it was not shorter, or smaller, but was squeezing more and more of its vile body within the broken skin of my palm. With my unaffected hand I began pressing along the wound, like you would a tube of toothpaste, in an attempt to force the wretched creature out of me, to no avail. A further attempt to squeeze it like a zit also failed. This wretched, filthy, vile thing was digging itself into my very skin, my body, my being. Quite suddenly, a rowboat appeared out of nowhere and I began to swim towards it. As I reached the side of the boat, I found a friend, a life long friend, manning the oars. I pulled myself up onto the side of the boat, resting my armpits on the edge, holding my painful hand with the uninjured one. My body and legs still dangling in the water, I again squeezed on either side of the wound in an effort to get a grasp on the vile being. Even amidst managing to get a couple of fingers on it, I was still unable to pull the worm out. As I pinched each side of the wound, pinning the worm in place, my friend came to the edge of the boat, grabbing onto what I could not grab. With an agony I had never experienced, and with the sound of a piece of spaghetti being sucked into someone's mouth, she pulled and the worm slid out of the wound. While relieved, the memory of the agony was not quickly forgotten as it pushed beyond the realm of purely the physical. An intensely deep mental and emotional anguish accompanied the very distasteful experience. I was forced within the deep recesses of my mind, and heart, as the very wound within my hand exposed my inner being, both to the breeding ground of infection and disease but also to the healing ability and power of engaging with another willing to join me in my pain.

The fascination and intrigue of human relationship, its most basic unit being friendship, has occupied much of my mind for many of my years. My very vivid dream, the one described above, pushed me even further into contemplation, and is the true beginning of this book. I have found my waking thought being preoccupied by relationships and how they work. I question closeness and intimacy and how it is cultivated. I question my importance to others and the importance others have to me. I find myself drawn to the painful parts as much as the ones that bring me joy and happiness. I carefully comb over the painful parts of human relationship. Why is it that we are so good at hurting each other? Possibly a better question might be, why am I so good at hurting others?

I often wonder why I am so inclined to do so; maybe it's because I fear relationship, maybe it's because I am bad at relationships, or maybe it's because I live life void of the relationship I need and was created for. I believe the latter to be overwhelmingly true. The more I engage in the relationships around me, the more I am inclined to believe that I cannot exist without them. My relationships have saved my life and have given me life, and I do not want to imagine the places I would be without them.

At the same time, part of me despises relationship. Being completely individual and independent is desirous and tempting. There are times when everything within me screams against connection to others; to not have any responsibility for or to the many others around me, doing what I want when I want and how I want.

But then, maybe I am scared. Scared of connection, and scared of how I may be challenged and pushed to become who I was created to be.   I guess it may seem strange to be scared of becoming who you are supposed to become but I have come to realize that true connection and relationship calls me into the deepest and darkest parts of myself; parts I avoid on the best of days.

For a time I simply thought that I was just growing into my adulthood and that these questions and pondering were by and far statements of growth and maturity. On second glance, relationships are constantly changing: from childhood to adolescence, from adolescence to adulthood, from adults with no children to adults with many children.   The relationships around me are constantly changing and constantly manifesting themselves in new ways. One of my most recent questions: How does a single unattached guy find himself within the married and children-filled realm of his friends? There are so many more questions that I feel have few answers. But, within the struggle of the questions, there is beautiful opportunity for growth and self-discovery. I have often wondered when this pondering of relationships will end but I have come to accept and embrace the never-ending journey that I have embarked on. I will never stop engaging with relationships and I will never stop learning within relationships. Within my human brokenness, I have perverted the truth of relationship and now I find myself hopefully caught within the responsibility of engaging and connecting with those around me. I must take on the challenge of this journey of self-discovery and exploration as it speaks of my human longing to be connected and loved.

To be connected, to love and be loved, is a basic human need and it pains me at times at how horrible I can be at it. I create distance and push away. I step too close and smother. I talk too much. I talk too little. With pride and arrogance I protect myself in stature. With meekness and timidity, I protect myself in being unknown. My human fragility and brokenness unavoidably tears into the fabric of my relationships and the connection I have to others. I am undoubtedly convinced the only way to the other side is straight through the pain of brokenness and fragility. Not alone, but within the relationships and connections that eagerly invite me to do so.

Within all of this, above all of this, is my connection to the Divine; the One who created me, knows the number of hairs on my head, loves me to death, and desires connection with me. And this is one of the most important things I have learned, and am learning, that found within my connection to the Divine is the connection I have to the people around me. The same hurt, pain, frustration, struggle, and lack of connection that I experience in my human relationships can be found in my connection to the Divine. On the other side of this is that the same love, joy, happiness, and intimacy that I experience in my human relationships can be found in my connection to the Divine. Or, maybe stated in a more appropriate way is that every relational dynamic I experience relates both to my connection to the Divine and my connection to the people around me. The everyday relationships I have point me toward the Divine, if I let them, and my everyday connection to the Divine points me toward the relationships around me, again, if I let them.

The closer this book gets to being in the hands of a reader, the more I become terrified. In writing this, I invite myself further into vulnerability, to intimacy, to openness, to relationship, to the Divine. People will see huge parts of me that I do not, and often cannot, allow myself to express or expose. Most recently I have become quite fond of the word delirium because often, as I find myself reflecting and writing, I realize how overwhelmingly biased my thoughts are in everyway, filtered through every life experience. I use the term delirium because I acknowledge how easily it is to be caught up in what I believe to be true to the point of completely disregarding the actual truth that is directly in front of me, almost as though living in a state of delirium. My mind, and I hope, for my own sake, any mind, can get so easily lost in the lenses we see our world through. The lens of a closed mind filters the brightness of life to a point that only small details can be amazingly vivid, and on the other side is an open-minded lens that permits the brightness of life to shine so vibrantly that important details become lost. And so, I invite you, my reader, into my delirium and I hope that somewhere along the way you can find a piece of yourself, a piece of others, and a piece of the Divine.

2

The Berlin Wall

I am sitting on the Berlin wall. Against my back is a spray-painted "East + West," along with a small peace sign. Opposing this positive message is the feel of the cold, hard concrete that is pressing against my back and buttocks, reminding me of the negative symbol that this wall once was; separation, division and control. The wall's crumbling in 1989 became a symbol of peace, hope, and freedom that re-united a country.

There are six slabs of the Berlin wall where I sit, at this random Nova Scotian location, all standing in a row with spaces between them, almost like six tombstones in a cemetery. At rest is the ideology and presence of control that these tombstones once exerted.

I find a part of myself here, as I sit on this slab of concrete history. I feel almost as if it were a cry against my very being not to come and spend time in this place. I got on a flight to come out here, not to see the Berlin wall as I did not know there was a piece of it here, but to both write and to visit. On the flight I picked up a book[1] that connected me with many thoughts and ideas that I have had for quite some time. The book challenged me to think outside of the box and to not be trapped by the plethora of voices that speak to me regarding whom I should and need to be, and more generally whom we should and need to be. Our lives, and who we are at our core, should not be controlled or manipulated by the world around us. This may sound quite logical and maybe not even profound but when we begin to look closer at the things causing us pain and frustration, we need to realize that sometimes, maybe even most times, we are not the problem but the system that we operate within, and have been raised in, is. Of course this does not relieve us from responsibility but inevitable invites us into the role of changing the system around us.

Maybe this is making no sense at all. Here is an example that we can all relate to; the pain of holding one's bladder. Without being painfully graphic, I know that everyone at some point or another knows the burning pain and desire of finding a washroom. Everyone also knows that adding coffee, or basically any caffeine, only adds to this burning pain and desire. This is where the thought comes together. I love sitting down with a cup of coffee and a friend. Something I have noticed is that many times when someone leaves to go to the washroom, the conversation gets interrupted and when the person returns from the washroom the suggestion to leave gets brought up and the wonderful dialogue that

---

[1] *The Paradigm Conspiracy*

was taking place ends. I suppose that there are many factors that could be thrown into this scenario, like time factors of needing to get to another appointment or engagement, but I noticed this occurrence and, because of this, I would often hold my bladder so tightly until I felt I was going to burst in the hopes of protecting and prolonging the wonderful dialogue I was enjoying. I was hurting myself and causing myself pain because the system I live in told me that when a conversation is temporarily broken, it provides the opportunity to leave regardless if the dialogue is complete or not, or regardless of whether the other person in conversation would like it to end. I eventually decided causing myself pain was quite ridiculous considering the burning pain and desire for a washroom distracted me from the conversation anyway. Instead, if faced with this situation I simply say, "I need to go to the washroom, are we going to leave if I do? Because I would like to continue this conversation."

The pain I experienced in keeping myself from the washroom was completely personal to me and I could have simply gone with the status quo of getting up to go to the washroom and risking the end of the dialogue. If the dialogue did in fact end I would simply need to let it end and then face the sadness of a misplaced connection in dialogue. However, in questioning and asking that we would stay and continue to dialogue after my return from the washroom, I go against the norm, or the system that we all have been a part of. My pain was not necessarily something I needed to simply deal with on my own, it was something to externalize, forcing me to engage with the system that enforced the pain. Sometimes pain is not simply something to deal with but something to externalize in an appropriate way, providing an opportunity to change the system that enforced the pain in the first place.

I need to talk a little more specifically about the book I read on the flight. Just as random as finding the Berlin wall in the middle of Nova Scotia was reading this book. About a week before my flight I visited a thrift store and came across this book, *The Paradigm Conspiracy: Why Our Social Systems Violate Human Potential – And How We Can Change Them,* by Denise Breton and Christopher Largent. I was only half drawn to this book but for a mere $2 I was sure it would look good on my shelf alongside the countless other books I have not read. As tradition beckoned as I packed, I began to go through my books and decide which ones I would bring, and I decided to place the current book in discussion in my carry-on bag. As the plane took off I decided to leaf through the book and find out what it was about. Two hundred pages later I decided that my perspective on life could not and should not be the same. Breton and Largent have pushed me to acknowledge or become more aware of the paradigms that I live within. Everything we do is based on a paradigm, basically a "map of reality – our worldview, life perspective, philosophy, or mental model" (Breton and Largent, *The Paradigm Conspiracy* 5). Added to this concept are the layers of paradigms that exist within one single life. I have my own paradigm on any given life situation or occurrence but on top of that I am a part of collective paradigms. I collectively contribute to my family's paradigm. For example, loudest person wins the conversation in my family and if you want to be heard you speak up, or yell, to be heard at times. I contribute to that paradigm by joining in, either by being loud, or by shutting up and letting others be loud. Beyond the paradigms within a family are the paradigms of larger

social structures: work, religion, or government. This is
where the rubber meets the road; if I am a part of society,
I have a part in shaping the paradigms that are around
me, whether I am realizing it or not, simply by going along
with it. And, if this is true, the delirium, my delirium, that
I have mentioned before, speaks not only of my own
paradigm but also is connected to the larger social
structures, from my family to organizations I am a part of:
my work, social group, church, government, and any
other social structure I participate in. So, in a sense, my
delirium speaks not only of myself but speaks of you as
well.

The book on the plane combined with my visit to the
Berlin wall here in the random location of Truro, Nova
Scotia has helped me step further into the discovery, and
understanding, of my delirium. I am learning my delirium
is not always just mine, but yours as well. We are in this
life together and all the pains we experience in
relationship, individually or collectively, invite us into an
opportunity to not only change ourselves but also the way
we all relate and interact in relationship. I could easily
face my pains and simply adjust to the world and its
norms, its paradigms or systems, and life could go on.
However, sometimes I realize that in my pain there is
something true that needs to be exposed and uncovered.
The Berlin wall stood as a societal norm for nearly thirty
years until the pain of a people in a broken country rose
up in protest. It was their collective voice that became
the driving force that brought the wall down. And I
suppose that this is one of my greatest hopes in writing
this book; that through the exposure of my pain and
frustrations, and through the wisdom of life around me,
that collectively the way we do relationship would be
shaped for the better.

3

The Beachcomber I am

The sea is an addiction. Like an overly realistic adult, I came to the beach of the Atlantic Ocean, books and laptop in tote, in the expectation that I would write pages and pages. Five hours later I feel like a playful child, with a bag full of rocks, shells, and seaweed in tote along with the disappointment of the overly realistic adult looming over my shoulder. The truth is I have not been to the ocean since I was a child and deep within me was nothing but a desire to be that playful child once again, so that is what I did. I needed to be honest with myself.

The other night I went for a late moonlit walk along this same beach. Along the way I picked up a bright looking object from the sand. I placed both it and my hand into my pocket and continued walking. I wondered what the object looked like as I played with it in my pocket and felt its crevices and cracks. I decided it was a small shell and as I walked, I continued playing with it wondering what it looked like. I decided there was something mysterious and wonderful about not knowing what it looked like. I was set on never looking at it. I would always keep it in my pocket and I would show others but I would never set gaze on it. It quickly became a symbol of myself as I thought about how it was almost like the pieces of myself that I often feel, even quite deeply, but can never see. Parts of myself that even get exposed so that they are visible, or evident, to others, but still not always to myself. Like how whiny and annoying I for surely am at times. This shell was going to remain in my pocket forever. I was going to use it as a reminder of how there are parts of me that remain unknown to myself but can often be so visible to others. I was already planning how I would avoid seeing it as I moved it out of one pocket to another or where I would store it if I had no pockets to pocket it in. I would have to find a special storage space for it. I would have to know exactly where it was at all times in case by chance I came across it exposed to my eye's view.

And then something happened. I was feeling the shell in my pocket and I decided there was great need to check how hard and strong it was so I pinched it hard between my fingers. It crushed into many broken pieces. I could tape it... or glue it maybe? No, I realized that this was ultimately what I wanted and longed for. I want to be able to see myself as others see me, the parts I feel but do not see of myself. When that shell snapped, I connected with the reality that I did not want invisible parts of myself exposed to everyone but me.

Honesty and openness are the closest words that I desire. In order to not have the visible parts of myself exposed to everyone but me someone or something has to tell me. I could read a book, listen to a song, go to a lecture, or anything else impersonal, and I could be forced to reflect on my life. For the most part, I feel that these somewhat impersonal channels are all that we rely on. On the other end of this is someone revealing the parts of ourselves that are invisibly exposed to us. I was talking with my friend Brendan about honesty and this is what he quite brilliantly stated, "No-one tells me when my breath stinks." I am sure when Brendan said this there was at least one occurrence that he had in mind. He was probably noticing people distance themselves as he talked with them. He may have even felt a little bit hurt or rejected because people avoided him. The uncommon trait of bad breath was invisibly exposed to Brendan. He had no clue he had bad breath and no one told him. I wonder if he came across a book in a library that discussed bad breath, forcing him to reflect on his own life of bad breath? It would have been nice if someone would have stepped in and simply told Brendan, for everyone's sake, really.

This example is clearly one of physical proportions. What of deeper things? Here is a story. My friend Tim and I took part in a momentous occasion in our friendship; one in which we have come to label as Drunken Night. As the label suggests, it was unfortunately a night of liquid debauchery. Alcohol has somewhat of a truth serum element to it and Drunken Night in many ways turned into a truth-telling time that I do not regret in the slightest. At one point during the evening my friend Tim and I were talking about a person we both know and that I somewhat have despised (I suppose we can add gossip to the night of debauchery). Within this conversation, or gossip, I had called this individual of topic fake when in all reality I hardly know the person. Tim looked at me and point blank said, "That's what you do Dustin, you sit down with a person and say, 'Okay whaddya gonna offer me? How honest and vulnerable are you gonna be? How real are you gonna be?' And then you give them about ten seconds and if they don't give you what you want you say 'Fuck You Then!'" This was harsh and ripped me almost to my core. It was true, maybe still is. Just like someone needed to tell Brendan that his breath stunk, I needed to be told that this is what I do. I do not want to be walking around handing out quick judgments of people based on how honest or vulnerable they can be within the first ten seconds. It's not fair to them or me.

It is mostly a shame that the social lubricant of alcohol was needed in order for this lesson to be learned. I may not have learned it otherwise and this saddens me. Where is the honesty I seek? I myself don't offer this honesty to others. We have created a system where honesty is limited. A roommate once asked me how I was doing and I told him straight up, "I am really stressed right now and I am struggling with some depression." His response was "Oh, isn't that something that a person should keep to himself?" Everything within me cries out and asks the reason why our honesty has to be limited to things like our favorite color or what we like to eat for breakfast. Honesty is limited. I suppose, however, that honesty does, or at least should, have limits. For example I would probably not tell a girlfriend that her hair looks horrible, unless maybe she asked.

We, you and I, and this culture, have limited honesty to the point of pain. Amongst doing therapy, doing art, and writing I also enjoy much of my time at a steakhouse as a server. There was one day in particular that I was being rather lazy, on top of which I was training a new staff member. I came up to a table and asked how things were going and this is the response I got, "I would like another ginger ale please, and just so you know the service is really, really slow." I was excitedly shocked. The bluntness and honesty caught me completely off guard and it amazed me. My response was "Thank-you, no one ever tells me when I am doing a crappy job. I appreciate that. I can totally pick up the pace here, my apologies." I was sincere in saying it because, as I talked with the table later, I expressed how most people would sit there being grumpy and never expressing that there was a problem. I was absolutely excited that this happened and I think the person I was training must have thought I was crazy considering the huge smile I had on my face as I elatedly talked about it afterwards. It seems that often we would rather suck it up and be angry, or be in some other sort of annoyance than to simply say something. I have seen numerous tables that become grumpy and I have not the slightest reason why. People will come in friendly and talkative and leave grumpy despite being asked how things are. Before I start making myself look like a horrible server, let me tell you I provide great service to 99.9% of my tables. Ego boost out of the way, this woman who complained about my slow service did a favor to both her and I. She was able to enjoy herself and not continually get hung up, and grumpy, on the fact that I was providing slow service and I got to be challenged and given the opportunity to change my behaviour. I do not want to be walking around offending people.

Now before I go on a rant about other people and how they need to be more honest, let me talk about myself. I love honesty and I really value when people can just tell it to me how it is but I know that I myself often stay grumpy and try to simply suck it up, pretending nothing is wrong. I know that I limit the connections with the people I have around me by not offering honesty as a gift.

At the same time I have a great gift and ability to be too honest. I had a friend once tell me the reason he stopped being friends with me was that I was too honest. This still completely baffles me as I have often racked my brain trying to figure out what part of the honesty was so offensive that I would lose a friend over it, and maybe, secondly, that if they were willing to tell me that it was my honesty, why they would not have expanded? Instead I am left in the dark. However, this is not my point. My point is that honesty is needed so badly at times within the realm I live in, it seems, at the same time, there needs to be some limits, a balance.

I was talking with my friend Pam and she suggested that honesty needs to be balanced with kindness. Just like I suggested that I would probably not tell a girlfriend that her hair looked horrible, there needs to be kindness within the honesty we share. I suppose it begs the question of what the purpose of the honesty would be. Does it pain me so much to look at her stupid, ugly, hideous hair that I need to tell her? If it is simply because I am embarrassed to be with her then it probably is not a good reason. However, if it is because we were going out on the town and she may feel embarrassed or would want to know her hair looked horribly ugly, maybe I should be honest and tell her. And then enter kindness. I would more than likely not use the words horribly ugly but replace them with something along the lines of a bit

out of place. The honesty that I would like to emulate
would be one that is appropriately delivered in the
kindest way possible.

. The other piece of this balance, I think, is that of
hiddenness. Henri Nouwen writes, "Just as words lose
their power when they are not born out of silence, so
openness loses its meaning when there is no ability to be
closed"(32). If we are too honest, the honesty becomes
meaningless. If we are so open in how we think and feel,
and nothing remains a mystery, the connections around
us have the ability to become boring and flat. This is one
part of too much honesty. The other part is that honesty
is overwhelming, especially within a system that does not
always value or respect honesty the way it should. This is
the piece I am not left in the dark about regarding the
friend who told me he stopped being friends with me
because I am too honest. Honesty can cut to the core and
if we offer too much, it can be crippling and defeating to
the receiver. I know that I overwhelmed my friend with
truth and honesty to the point of him not really knowing
what to do with it all. I regret this and it pains me that I
have seemingly lost such a valuable friend over something
as this. Hindsight is 20/20 and I know that there was a
place for me to communicate the things I did to my friend
but maybe not all at once and maybe not without
allowing him time to process it all.

Honesty balanced with kindness and hiddenness is
one that I know I need. I do not want to walk around
doing things that offend people or hurt people. I do not
want people to write me off because I am offensive, too
honest, or because I may give people ten seconds to make
a good impression on me. I want to be challenged and
learn, and grow further into the person the Divine One

created me to be because I know He did not create me to be annoying, over-bearing, or judgmental. I could read a book or listen to self-help tapes and maybe I will find the wisdom I need but what a resource and wealth of knowledge and wisdom there is in the people around me that I connect with. In the Bible it says that, "As iron sharpens iron, so one man sharpens another" (*NIV*, Proverbs 27:17). I want this.

I talked to my friend Michelle about this and I later texted her, "Do you think that we could handle the kind of abrasive friends that you and I said we wanted?" This is what she said, "It would take time but yes." I believe my friend Michelle, as she is quite wise, nice too. It will take an adjustment and will mean shifting the way I think. It will also require some vulnerability.

4

Pizza With a Homeless Man

I randomly found myself enjoying a slice of pizza with a homeless man one night. I just happened to be hungry as I left work and was stopped by a homeless man, who I later found out was named Ryan, asking for money for food. As we all know, addiction is a huge problem on the street so I naturally questioned myself about whether I should offer him some money. I decided to invite him to have something to eat with me instead. We ended up at a pizza place. I began to ask him get-to-know-you questions. I asked him what he did during the day and he told me that he tried to save money to buy things, and then made a brief comment about needing money for an addiction. Being the inquisitive therapist I am, I probed, "What kind of addiction?"

He looked at me, lifted his hands in a motion of defense and said, "Hey man, don't judge me."

"Heck no," was my immediate response. I began to ignorantly think about why a homeless man, of all people, would be worried about people judging him.

"Well… morphine. I get a hit in the morning, one at night, and then I drink as well… drinking, that's my thing." He again mumbled something about being judged or judgment in general.

"You are no different than anyone else, we all struggle," I replied.

Caught in the acknowledgement of his own humanity, he looked at me awkwardly and said, "Thank-you for the pizza. I have to go," as he swiftly walked out the door.

Ryan was exposed, almost as if he were standing naked in front of me. He told me very personal information and most likely fearing rejection, he simply left the conversation. I wonder how the conversation would have gone if he had not made the decision to quickly leave.

I got into my car and began to drive home. As some annoying pop tune was playing on the radio I thought of Ryan and a portrait of my own life snapped into reality. I am much like Ryan at times. I do not like to be exposed and I tend to avoid such situations accordingly. For the most part, I remain quite guarded so that no one has the ability to see something they may not like. Ultimately, I do not want anyone to think ill of me or judge me. I hold my cards close enabling myself to easily create a confident and collected persona, or façade, that most people don't have the privilege of seeing past. I can appear to have my life together in every aspect and no

one will be the wiser. And, to be honest, I have been
quite successful, at times, with this persona. Someone
once told me that they would have befriended me but
that I appeared very confident, collected, and that I really
had no more room or space for a new friend. It breaks
me to think that a persona would keep me from
connecting with the wonderful people around me. Fear
of vulnerability results in lost connections and fake
friendships based on superficial fluff. Fear of vulnerability
has demanded satisfaction with surface relationships that
only leave me thirsting for the deep. I know the deep,
have felt the deep, experience the deep, but from day to
day I sometimes wonder where it is.

The sad truth is that I do not think I am alone in this.
I think many of us greatly fear the exposure of our true
humanity. I am talking about the real grit; the pain, the
lack of confidence, fear, and doubt. In Jean Vanier's book
Becoming Human, he writes, "There is a lonely child in
each of us, hidden behind the walls we created in order to
survive" (20). I think we are scared of this lonely child.
We are not sure if we like this child and we are scared
about what others may think if they knew this lonely
child. So, instead of spending time getting to know this
child, we, as Vanier states, build a wall around ourselves.
We become confident and secure in the wall and, rarely,
if ever, take the time to nurture the lonely child within us.

I finished the previous chapter talking about how the
honesty I want will require some vulnerability. This is the
vulnerability I am talking about. In order to have the
honesty I crave, I am going to have to be able to face that
inner lonely child with open arms and embrace him for
whoever he is. I need to stop taking comfort and solace
in the wall I have created, the persona.

This will mean many things, above much it will risk appearing weak. For example, I used to especially be careful about telling people that I appreciated them or that I liked hanging out with them because I did not want to ever risk the appearance that I was hard up for friends or that I really needed a connection with them. At the same time, I was not honest when people hurt me because I feared that to admit being hurt I would come off as weak or too sensitive.   For the sake of my confident persona, I had to ignore many of the lonely child's cries.

And so, I will cry and appear weak. I will fucking swear and appear immature. I will yell and appear insane. I will remain silent and appear stupid. I will laugh and appear out-of-control. I will do what it takes to simply be who I am created to be. I will not put on a façade and I will not be who I am not.

Sigh, but yes I will, my society tells me I have to. I cannot cry and appear weak. I cannot swear and I will exude maturity. I will be complete, lacking nothing. I cannot yell or appear insane. I will speak up in defense of my superior intellect. I cannot laugh or appear out-of-control. I will always be calm, cool, and collected because that's what people expect and that's what people look up to, and even praise. I will raise my nose in pride and I will walk on. I will sacrifice myself for the sake of being what others want or expect.

I am brought to tears at the fakeness I am at times. I am also brought to tears over the society that has allowed me and even encouraged me to be this way. I want to live honestly and be honest. I want to be as weak as I am weak in any given moment, and as strong as I am strong in any given moment. It seems, at times, however, that in order to be a successful, respected, and looked-up to individual, I have to pretend. I can be very good at pretending but I am sick of it. I have often felt like I am in the eternal state of a job interview, always talking about how great I am, what I have to offer, and pretending to be the greatest person around, proving that I have what it takes to be a successful friend.

Another part of me feels like the character Holden Caulfield in *The Catcher in the Rye* by J.D. Salinger. I could easily see myself in this character. Holden Caulfield is often disgusted with the fakeness he sees around him. His whole existence seems to scream for true connection to the point of allowing the practical things in life to simply crumble. I roll my eyes, I scoff, I get judgmental, I cringe but mostly I am drawn into a deep melancholy because I know there is more out there. I know there is a more honest and vulnerable way of being; one that will open me, and all of us, to a fuller way of life. As I expose myself to this possibility, I find glints of reality in the connections around me. I also find true connections. And, at the same time, I find glints of despair in the lack of connections around me or lack of ability for connection.

I am terrified to be caught like a morphine addicted homeless man in a pizza place. I hesitate to share areas of struggle out of fear of judgment. With great trepidation I share my hopes and dreams because if they become unattained, I risk appearing a failure. I fear sharing my beliefs or opinions in case I get proven wrong. I think that I, and probably a general we, often hold back from saying the things we need to say. Somehow I seem to wait for the most odd and out of the blue occasions to express what I need to say. I wait until life falls apart. I only tell people I appreciate them when crises happen. I wait for moments of chaos and turmoil to share the things I should have already shared. I will wait for the last possible second in a coffee meeting to divulge the real things I want to talk about. I stay within the status quo as much as possible in order to remain as collected and together as I can for the longest possible amount of time.

On the other side of my connections are the people that do express their vulnerability to me. You may think that with my frustration with the seeming fakeness around me that vulnerability would be an ever-welcome friend. It is not always. To hear and engage with another's vulnerability forces me to a place within my own vulnerability and sometimes that place is not a place I like to venture. And again, it becomes about not wanting to be caught like a morphine addicted homeless man in a pizza place and fear cripples the connection.

There is more than this. I deserve more than this. We deserve more than this. I was getting off the train one day and I was in a rush as it was a busy day and I had a lot of errands to do. As I was stepping off the train and as the doors were sliding closed behind me, a mentally challenged man was running onto the platform hoping to catch the train before it departed for its next destination. He was clearly going to miss it. He was frantic and was making a loud moaning sound in desperation as he waved his hands in the air. He missed the train. I heard people giggling and I saw people staring, which I suppose included me. As I thought about his unfortunate circumstance of missing the train and the reaction he had, it occurred to me that he was probably the most real person out of everyone standing on the platform. I was in a rush and I had things to do. I wanted to get places and, in reality, was feeling a bit frantic myself. Instead of visually showing it, or expressing it, I bottled it up with a façade of calm and collected pride. There was something freeing in this man's behaviour that I craved. He was as real as his inner being told him and as expressive as his inner being communicated.

For years I have protected and covered much of my realness from others. I suppose I still do. I have worked very hard at creating a very confident and secure persona, and as I have mentioned I feel I have been quite successful. However, I am for surely never as successful as I would like. I once went to a counselor and this is how the conversation went:

"You are transparent," said the counselor.

"No I am not, I hide my problems," was my immediate and somewhat angered response.

"Yes, and that is why you are transparent."

"No, I am not! I hide my problems, no-one can see them."

It makes me laugh to think about my lack of self-awareness in that moment because, looking back, there was something about the person I created myself to be that was not quite right. It was not true or real but a façade that held me back from the true connection I needed and need. There should be no need for me to have any façade. I want to be exactly who I am created and meant to be at any given moment and yet, I catch myself unknowingly hiding, backing away, and becoming less honest, less vulnerable. It is in these times that I realize I am terrified. I am terrified I will be taken the wrong way, misunderstood, or missed. So instead of taking the risk, I put up façades becoming what I perceive the world around me desires and takes pride in.

I can embellish, exaggerate, and flat out lie in order to be perceived in a way that the world around me would like, and I often do.

> In fact, psychologists have found the mirroring of opinions, even at the cost of the truth, to be a very common strategy for ingratiating oneself with others. The reasoning behind such behavior is rather straightforward. Most people shy away from conflict and disagreement. They build relationships with others based on fundamental things they have in *common*. In order to form a relationship with another person, then, one would want to avoid the areas of dissonance and emphasize the commonalities. (Feldman 18)

I suppose it makes sense that we would highlight, or exaggerate, similarities in order to develop friendships but something about doing this does not sit right with me. If I exaggerate and emphasize certain parts of myself, I am putting a false sense of self forward.

This is how I see these sorts of things playing out. I would exaggerate and expand the truth of who I am to fit in and, in the process, would begin to lose myself. I'd become more and more distant from who I am as I continue to live the lies I put forth until one day I cannot do it anymore and the relationships I have built around these lies crumble because they were based on lies. Ultimately I am left in my fear of being taken the wrong way, misunderstood, or missed. I put up a façade in an attempt to not be misunderstood or missed and, because of it, I am misunderstood and missed.

The funny, strange, or frustrating part of this all is that apparently "there's a clear connection between skill in lying and more general social aptitude, at least for adults. For adults, good liars also tend to be good at forming friendships, to be more empathic, to have greater social insight" (Feldman 74). I have made many attempts over the years to climb the social ladders around me, wanting to be accepted and liked. If I had only known that all it takes is a little bit of lying, it would have been a whole lot easier. I say this facetiously because what this says to me is that the human need to belong and be accepted is so great that we will do almost anything to get it, even if it means sacrificing who we truly are. I have done this and still do this on occasion. It feels good to be on the top of the social ladder, feeling accepted, even if I am not truly being myself. I get to feel strong, confident, well-liked, and if I am completely honest with myself, superior and better than everyone else that is not in the social position that I am in.

I don't want this because I also know that my human mind can be easily corrupted and living out parts of my life that are not true will do just that. "Screening what others know of us, we end up screening what we know of ourselves. Defensive shields come between us and our own reality, as we start believing the half-truths we put out" (Breton and Largent, *Paradigm Conspiracy* 81). As I choose to put half-truths forward and live a façade, I will begin to only see myself as the façade that I created. Having done this, I will grow further and further from the person I was created and meant to be, leading me to a life that I was not meant to live. I will be dulled into the commonalities that make me like everyone else and the uniqueness of who I am will be lost. And, if we all do this, even just a little bit, we all begin to miss out on the gifts that we are to each other. I will never fully discover the truth that you convey in your uniqueness and you will never fully discover the truth that I convey in my uniqueness.

5

Peas in a Pod to Snowflakes

Quite awhile back now I was having a rotten day and was feeling so disconnected to the world around me. I hadn't talked to anyone the whole day, except for maybe the Tim Horton's employee when they asked me how I wanted my coffee. I was, in the plainest sense of the word, lonely. I started to wonder if anyone understood me or understood my life. I had just happened to be walking outside and it was snowing. For some reason, I started to think about the snowflakes falling and how at some young age I was taught the lesson that every snowflake is different and that there are no two the same, and how it applied to all of us humans. At the very moment I was walking outside thinking about this snowflake lesson, I hated it. I did not like the idea of being a snowflake that was unlike the rest of the snowflakes. I just wanted to be another pea in the pod. If I was just another pea in the pod everyone would understand me completely and I would understand everyone else completely. There would never be any conflict between people because we would all understand each other. Honesty and vulnerability would be so simple and easy because we would all be in the same boat, or pea pod. Judgment, condemnation, and prejudice would crumble as we would all be the same. We would have the same struggles, the same joys, the same strengths, and the same weaknesses. I would be witness to a great world of commonality.

It would be great until we realized there would be nothing to talk about, nothing to learn, and no one to be challenged by. Within our collective commonality the mundane would overwhelm us. As I thought more about the falling snowflakes, I realized that it was more than okay being a snowflake, in fact I invited it. Through the interaction with the world around myself, especially with those that I am close to, I cannot only become aware of my similarities but also how much I am different and this is one of the greatest things ever.

It is one of the greatest things ever because it is where I am different and experience my uniqueness, my snowflakeness, that I have the opportunity to connect with the Divine. Where others do not understand me, the Divine understands me, as vague as that may sound. When I experience difference and when I feel misunderstood, lonely, or lost in weakness it can be the best thing for me because it is in those moments that I realize my connection to the Divine all the more. I am told that the Divine knit me in my mother's womb (Psalm 139: 13) and that He knows the number of hairs on my head (Matthew 10:30). I choose to believe that He is more than able to understand me. The connection with the Divine, I believe, becomes the Biblical analogy regarding a potter and his clay. In meeting the Divine in my uniqueness, I allow Him to enter into my life in such a way that He shapes and molds me into who I am truly meant to be.

From here, the connection that I develop with the Divine One outpours to the people around me. As I become the piece of pottery that the One has and is shaping me to be, I become a gift to others. And likewise, as you meet the One in embracing your differences, you become a gift to me. The mutual gift becomes one of admiration, inspiration, and challenge. Instead of simply meeting each other in our likeness and commonality, talking about sports or how much we like sushi, we embrace our differences and challenge, encourage, and inspire each other.

As I think more about what I am writing here and about my snowflakeness, I realize that I am talking about two different things. I need to distinguish and elaborate on these two snowflake components, because the snowflakeness that I can and do experience is two-fold. It is everything about me in the way I was created that makes me different than anyone else. It is also everything within my brokenness and weakness that makes me different or at least feel different.

Intrinsic Differences

I am calling the differences that are simply a result of being created as a unique person intrinsic differences. Intrinsic in that the differences speak of who I am at my core and meant to be. To those who I feel are intellectual, I will put on my intellectual persona. To those that are silly and goofy, I can pull out a goofy and silly persona. I am not saying that I am not these things but I feel that I can often exaggerate parts of myself to the point of creating a bit of a façade.

Salvador Dali, a twentieth century surrealist artist, talks about these differences as being a part of his creative genius. Written in his biography is this:

> Most human beings seemed like wretched wood lice to me, crawling about in terror, unable to live their lives with courage enough to assert themselves. I deliberately decided to emphasize all aspects of my personality, and exaggerate all the contradictions that set me that much more apart from common mortals. (Dali and Parinard 47)

Too often I find myself simply trying to adjust to the world around me, attempting to fit in and find my place, that I end up sacrificing the trueness of who I am. I become a walking projection of the things and people around me, falling into social expectations and roles. Lost is the true gift that I am to the world around me. That may sound quite arrogant but I know and realize that all of you have the potential to be a great gift to me and sometimes I am sad because we completely miss each other in the reality of always meeting each other in our commonalities.

Dali chose to simply stand against social conformity and embraced everything that was different about himself. What he found in doing so was a creative genius that has provided much to the art world. I spent two hours reveling at his work at a gallery in London and I was brought to many different places within my mind to the point of being told when I left the gallery that I looked like I was bathed in inspiration.

Salvador Dali found a creative genius within the intrinsic differences of who he was. I think that same ability can and is found within all of us. I want this and I need this. There is something within the way I was created that allows me to find a piece of truth, even the Divine, if I embrace my uniqueness, so that I can then in turn give back to the people around me that have the potential to, and do, honor me with the same gift.

I have a friend who chooses to keep much of his inner and personal life quite close to him. He was my closest friend for a while but our friendship got to a point where it seemed I was not allowed to come any closer. The analogy of a long corridor with a door at the end of it was brought into conversation. The door was the entryway into everything he holds close to him, from pain and hurt to things of joy and happiness. He told me that no one is in the door. I was saddened, both for him and me. I was sad for him because he does not need to live life so alone. I was sad for myself because in him living so closed, I feel that he was keeping me from the gift that he truly is. Maybe the irony is that the very fact he lives this way is a difference, one that I can learn from and even be blessed by.

Weakness and Brokenness

Closely related to my craving and desire for more vulnerability, as I expressed earlier, is my craving and desire for the openness to weakness. No one can claim my individual pains, struggles, and hurts, at least in the same way that I can. There is something about my weakness and brokenness that makes it mine and makes me unique. In the same way I want, and even need, to embrace my intrinsic differences I also want, and even need, to embrace my weakness and brokenness.

Salvador Dali also speaks of this aspect of life when he writes that his "soul battens on what crushes it and finds sublime orgasm in what denies it. Weakness itself becomes strength, and I am enriched by my contradictions. I live with eyes lucid and wide open, unashamed, without remorse, and emerge as a spectator of my own existence" (Dali and Parinard 13). In embracing the painful parts of life, Dali finds a strength that takes him beyond himself to the point of being a spectator of his own existence. His life stretches beyond himself. Encapsulated in this is a profound and deep sense of self-acceptance, complimenting Jean Vanier's wisdom that "[o]nly when all our weaknesses are accepted as part of our humanity can our negative, broken self-images be transformed" (*Becoming Human* 26).

Sexual connotations aside, I have been called a sadist at times for the amount I will hold onto painful pieces of my life, dwelling in the darkness. I will analytically dwell in the darkest of places, causing not only myself pain but sometimes, or often, those close to me. I have unfortunately even lost a very dear friend because of it. Part of me likes to think that if I hold onto the things that hurt me long enough that they will eventually not hurt anymore. If I can figure out what it is that hurts, the root, I can rid my life of it indefinitely. For the amount of pain I have held onto, I am still unsure if this is an absolute truth. At the same time I am unsure that I regret holding onto any of the pain that I have experienced as my eyes and heart have been opened to priceless truths that I may have never stumbled upon otherwise. Again, at the same time I am not sure I recommend it, as it is definitely not for those weak of heart, most likely me being one of them.

However, this is what I have experienced. As I have grappled with, and held onto the pains I experience, it connects me with something larger. My pain becomes a picture not only of my own life but also of those around me. My hurt and brokenness is simply an echo, or extension, of the pain and brokenness found within the world. Empathy, compassion, and love for the people around me becomes inevitable. "Seeing our own brokenness and beauty allows us to recognize, hidden under the brokenness and self-centeredness of others, their beauty, their value, and their sacredness" (Vanier, *Becoming Human* 159). So, as I step into my pain and brokenness I also invite myself to reflect on the pain I see around me and, as Dali says, I become a spectator of my own existence or, better said, our existence.

Too often we build friendships and communities solely on commonality and strength, ignoring the differences and weakness. "I like sushi, you like sushi, and we both want world peace, lets be friends forever. And let's never talk about the fact that we both are imperfect." All I know is that I get exhausted of simply being similar, and fully collected at any given moment. I have learned how to highlight the appropriate strengths, or commonalities, at the appropriate times. I have learned to be socially polite, courteous, and gracious at times when everything inside of me is screaming out in pain, or frustration. Why can't I just be who I am and you be who you are? Why do we have to hide behind the things we are good at or who we want to be known as?

I create and I think we create these personas of strength that blind ourselves from the true reality of the human life around us. Jean Vanier writes, "We all tend to wear masks, the mask of superiority or of inferiority, the mask of worthiness or of victim. It is not easy to let our masks come off and to discover the little child inside of us who yearns for love and for light, and who fears being hurt" (*Becoming Human* 158). At the cost of dragging a ball and chain of weakness, pain, and brokenness that keeps us from being fully who we are created and meant to be, we wear masks of superiority, confidence, and strength. In the act of always putting our best foot forward, only showing the best that we are, we create a society that only sees strength. We begin to lose, or neglect, a part of ourselves, the lonely and vulnerable child that is inside of us. Forgetting that weakness and vulnerability are part of simply being human, we exert our power and strength. And when the lonely inner child gets neglected for long enough a heart wrenching scream comes forth, "You aren't good enough … you need to do better … what a failure you are."

It becomes almost impossible to be weak, despite the fact that we all have weakness. We create subcultures of people that are not quite good enough, often labeling them as burdens on society: The poor, the needy, the mentally or physically challenged, the elderly, or the unlovable. These people simply do not measure up and so they are cast aside while the rest of us attempt to take part in the competing strength competition of our society, asking, challenging and enslaving ourselves with the same question that Snow White's evil stepmother continually asked, "Mirror, mirror on the wall, who is the fairest of them all?"

This competitive and strength driven societal norm segregates and tempts us to wedge even the smallest of divisions into the greatest of our relationships, asking us to prove ourselves and be worthy. In a strength idealized world, it is more difficult to express vulnerability and brokenness. Admitting imperfection in a seemingly perfect world is not an easy thing to do. Admitting fault, sharing weakness, and exposing our brokenness to another can at times seem like the equivalent of being a sub-par human being. Shame runs rampant because the world tells us we have to be perfect and when we are not in the smallest of areas we fear rejection or worse experience it. Then, in turn, we push away and reject those smallest of areas, ignoring the self-acceptance, love, and light that those areas need.

We deserve more than to be blinded from reality. I do admit, living with differences, embracing them, and being vulnerably open is maybe harder but I truly believe that we are meant and created to highlight each other's differences and weaknesses. Where I am weak and broken, there is an invitation for you step closer and bless me with your strength, but only if I let you see my broken and weak parts. In this way my weakness becomes a gift of closeness to you and your strength a gift to me. It is within the deepest recesses of our minds, hearts, and souls, that there is something unique and special of ourselves to offer those around us. You are a gift to me, and I am a gift to you. Somehow we need to find a way to share the gifts that we are.

6

It's the End of the World

The Feeling of Being Dreadfully Alone

Probably a year or so ago I phoned my Baba to see how she was doing. She was quite quick to tell me about her recent experience of witnessing a meteor falling to the ground. She elatedly told me both the factual details as well as her immediate reaction to the event. "It was as big as a moon and I said out loud to myself, 'Oh my God, it's the end of the world and I'm here alone in my house.'" This statement, probably for a couple of reasons, immediately struck me. First, it seemed ridiculous that she would be concerned about being alone because if it was indeed the end of the world, what would it matter? The second and possibly more profound thought was the realization of how alone my Baba lives and how lonely it must be at times. She lives year long in a lakeside cabin, which becomes quite desolate during the winter. I started to wonder about what this must be like, if she was lonely, and how lonely, meteor striking or not.

It would only be a couple of months later, with the marriage of an ex-girlfriend as a trigger, that I realized how lonely I was myself. At first I was not even sure what to name what I felt. This what I wrote in my journal:

> *What is this pain I feel? This pit of despair? It is a dark place. I have my eyes wide open and I can't even make out a shadow or a shape of any sort. It's as if I had no vision at all. There is no sound. I hear nothing even though I am straining my ears, even a faint unclear whisper would be nice. But yet at the same time there seems to be a loud screaming that drowns out everything else. It is a tormenting painful cry. I think its coming from my own voice. My stomach is tight and in knots. There is no hope for anything because there is nothing. I feel deeply buried in adversity and challenged to the point of being numb.*

I remember this time quite distinctly; arm chair, dim lamp-lit room, box of an apartment, silence, and tears. James Frey compliments this distinct memory that is etched in my mind in his book, *A Million Little Pieces*:

> I hate that I have no one to talk to, I hate that I have no one to call, I hate that I have no one to hold my hand, hug me, tell me everything is going to be all right. I hate that I have no one to share my hopes and my dreams with, I hate that I no longer have any hopes and dreams, I hate that I have no one to tell me to hold on, that I can find

them again. I hate that when I scream, and I
scream bloody murder, that I am screaming into
emptiness. I hate that there is no one to hear my
scream and that there is no one to help me learn
how to stop screaming. (79)

As I re-read this quote right now, I wonder if one of my
favorite authors Jean Vanier is right in saying that
loneliness "can only be covered over, it can never actually
go away" because I am not sure that the pain described in
my journal above is truly gone (*Becoming Human* 7). I
think, somewhere, the same feelings of isolation are
hidden within who I am and how I experience life. They
are echoed in the question my Baba asks almost every
time I call her, "Do you have a girlfriend?" To be honest, I
am not sure at this point in my life, maybe ever, that I
want a girlfriend, or marriage, and I am almost certain
that I do not want children either but for some reason or
another in my Baba asking me this question there is a
small but present pang of loneliness every time I am
asked. The question was once followed by the statement,
"This life is a lonely life. Everybody needs somebody."
This statement scares me because I cannot help but
wonder what this woman in her eighties knows about the
life ahead of me. Do I need to worry? Do I need to equip
myself with numerous friends? A wife? Children?

Balanced with this fear and cry of loneliness is my
deep longing and need to be alone and have solitude. I
know that there is also something within who I am that
screams for people to give me space. I can remember
being in grade six, a shy and quiet but happy child,
choosing to move my desk to be by the window alone,
even after being invited by another child, Brent, to be a
part of the other numerous children moving their desks

together. I truly loved my space by the window, even as, or just as, the other children enjoyed being closely socially connected. I know that I love spending hours alone and there is a part of me that comes completely alive in doing so. I have read books about mystics and people that live outside social conformity and norms that bring life and love to those around them. There is something about their lives I find to be admiringly appealing, not easy but appealing. Could I be one of these people? Maybe I just need to step further into this beautiful solitude.

These are the things I know. I don't look for friends. I have a habit of not seeking out friends. I hold most people at bay. I hold a very strong wall up and I am unsure if it is because I don't want more friends, my loner and introverted nature coming forth, or if it's because I absolutely fear rejection and have given up hope that any person can enter into and understand the delirium that I am. This is balanced by the fact that I refuse to let many get close to me because I know I do not want to make time for too many people. People are an investment and I don't have time for everyone, and I like my time alone. Although my fear is that I have indeed simply succumbed to fear and have simply accepted a lie that I am meant and created to be alone. I have learned that a person can learn to deal with and overcome much pain. We are quite resilient creatures. The problem is that our resiliency often calls on every resource we have which unfortunately can mean resorting to unhealthy patterns of relating or being. In order to make it through, we sometimes have to shut ourselves down, create distance, build walls, take shelter and hide. I hope I am not doing this, lying to myself and justifying the pain that needs to be healed.

The reality is I know for a fact there is probably at least a small piece, maybe even a big piece, that is using justification. And this is the fact, stated jeopardy style, "Why would I write a book discussing human connection and the lack of connection I feel if I was not lonely?" And I suppose this question answers my question. I am lonely. I am lonely but from the pain of my loneliness and from the knowledge of who I think and know I am, I am almost certain that I believe that the connection that I want or need is not out there. Again, my pain screams out in a belief that I hope I can discover not to be true. Maybe it's because I feel I am continually hurt and continually broken by the people around me when all I am attempting to do is love them the best way I know how. To leave myself out of the hurting and breaking of people is ridiculous because I know I do it too. I don't think I am alone in either of these situations but I think true friends are hard to find. There have been times it has been hard to find someone I could call a friend, let alone a true one. It is one thing to have a friend to talk about the latest movie or sports game, it is another to have one that will cry with you and not turn away and run when your brokenness begins to break through the façade we all create ourselves to be. Or to have one that is maybe okay for you to share your brokenness but runs at the sight of their own. Again, I say that I don't think I am alone in this because I know that I have been both types of these friends. I have hurt people deeply and I have been hurt deeply. I have run from friendship that exposed myself and I have also run from friendship that exposed my friendly counterpart. It is uncomfortable but it is also something I crave at the deepest level.

If people were to look at my life from an outsider's perspective I am sure that they would say I had a lot of friends, and I suppose this is true. I do have a lot of people that I could call up at any given moment and I could probably fill my time quite easily. If you looked solely at how I spend my time it probably would not be considered lonely but there is still something in my soul that screams of loneliness. I read that "[l]oneliness is a part of being human, because there is nothing in existence that can completely fulfill the needs of the human heart." (Vanier, *Becoming Human* 7). However, if there is nothing in this existence that can fully meet the needs of the human heart, I would like to at least meet the needs as much as this existence offers me. I want life to the fullest. And then it comes back again to the question, so how will I know if I am simply trying to convince myself that I am meant to be alone, created to be alone or that I truly am alone and lacking and wanting and even needing a true connection with those around me? I have decided that it is outside of my capacity to immediately answer this and that time will tell. If I am living as I am truly created and meant to be, my life will bring forth fruit. It says in the Bible that "[t]he one who sows to please his sinful nature, from that nature will reap destruction; the one who sows to please the Spirit, from the Spirit will reap eternal life" (Galatians 6:8). There is another piece of scripture that I am reminded of right now. It talks about living by the Spirit and, in doing so, love, joy, peace, patience, kindness, goodness, faithfulness, gentleness and self-control will come to fruition. My theory is that my question will be answered as I begin to watch the way I live produce fruit in my life. If all I get is bitter lemons then I know that something will need to change. Perhaps make lemonade, hmm? For now, I will reflect further on the great and the awful of loneliness as I have learned much from this often life-sucking feeling.

Alone + No Friends ≠ Loser

Too often I think I have associated the word 'loser' with 'lonely' because sometimes when loneliness strikes, immediate questions like, "What is wrong with me?" or "Why is it that I don't have friends?" pops into my head. I have learned to dismiss these questions because they are bullshit questions. When it comes down to it, why should anyone around me decide whether I am important or not?

When I shared my journal piece about feeling lonely, I recognized that I was not at first sure how to label the feeling I was experiencing. I have come to realize that I did not know how to name what I felt because I had always made myself busy with the people and things around me. This was a time in my life when the freedom and exhilaration of early adulthood, where and when people and places change almost weekly, was coming to an end. I was no longer a full-time student and life was beginning. I relied greatly on people to come and go, and come and go again, never having to really worry about developing real friendships and relationships. This came to a signified end when, as I mentioned above, an ex-girlfriend got married. This brought my loneliness to conscious awareness; there were few people that I could rely on regularly, if at all. I questioned. I began to question everything about my life and I was an anxious and lonely wreck for over a month with horribly clingy and annoying phone calls to almost anyone who would listen. I was eventually brought to that dark moment on the armchair, the darkest moment of conscious awareness of my loneliness. The clingy phone calls had to stop so I chose to sit there alone. I journalled, cried, wept, journalled, and wept more. I began to ask myself and the God who I am told saved me why I had to go through this? Why was I feeling this? Tears began to fade as a peace settled on me as I pondered what made me less human or less important because I was sitting here alone? Did the number of friends in my life equal my value or importance? Did the lack of connection I felt make me any less lovable? The answer was a resounding NO. How could anyone outside my own head, or in my living environment, see the full value or importance I have or fully see how much there is of me to love? Or how much love I have to offer? Just because people don't always notice or see the love I offer and the love I am created to be does not mean it's not true or does not exist. It became a clear choice for me to step out of the very dark, self-doubting questions.

There is a Biblical story of a man named Job. One day all his sons and daughters were killed in a wind storm. In Job's grief over this incident, after tearing his robe, he says, "Naked I came from my mother's womb, and naked I will depart. The Lord gave and the Lord has taken away; may the name of the Lord be praised." I am fairly certain that I would not be as gracious if this happened to me. I am actually quite certain that I would be dropping f-bombs right, left, and center. Apart from the profanity, I find something that makes me sigh in Job's words. The most important people in my life can be removed and my original state of being remains the same; naked I came from my mother's womb and naked I will depart. Just because Job had children, it made him no more or less important or valuable. Just as I have or don't have people in my life, it does not make me any more or less important or valuable. So, no longer is it worth my time to associate loser with lonely. I can feel lonely and it is simply another of the many human emotions that I allow myself to feel.

Loneliness is Beautiful in the Eye of the Beholder

I am not sure why but a part of me has been afraid to find out that I was, or am, lonely, even though a part of me knew it and knows it. I did not want to be a loser. It seemed weak to admit it and yet, I read that to feel lonely is something common to the human experience and if this is the case why should I be concerned with being what I am, a human? Apparently "[e]arly humans were more likely to survive when they stuck together, evolution reinforced the preference for strong human bonds by selecting genes that support pleasure in company and produce feelings of unease when involuntarily alone" (Cacioppo and Patrick 15). Loneliness has been programmed into my genes, so the fact that I feel lonely is something intrinsic in how I was created and it keeps me connected and a part of this human existence. I was created not to be alone. Eve was created for Adam because "it is not good for man to be alone" (Genesis 2:18). These two statements being made, I cannot rightfully deny that a part of me is lonely because in admitting that I am lonely is simply a statement about how my whole existence screams for the connection that I was created to have. Just as my stomach gurgles and grunts when I am hungry, my soul screams in pain when I lack connection.

Loneliness cannot be something that makes me wonder if I am a loser. It has instead begun to speak to me about how I need people in my life to keep me on the right path and that I can't do life alone, nor should I. There is something quite redeeming in knowing that loneliness keeps me connected to others because I am almost certain if it weren't for the feeling of loneliness, I would be a hermit living on a beach somewhere in a tropical country with my own cult-like religion, eating locusts and honey.

So, I will not be ashamed of being lonely, just as I should not be ashamed when I feel sad, happy, or hungry. It says nothing of my importance but everything about how I was created. If I am lonely it tells me two things; it reminds me that I am important outside of and apart from everything around me, and that I have something that no-one else has: In the simplest of words, my unique existence. Second, it tells me that other people have something to offer me and I have something to offer them. Loneliness is a built in reminder or motivator to keep me in connection to others.

There is one more piece of loneliness that I find wretchedly beautiful. Loneliness, like few other things, has the ability to cut me to my core and expose me to one of my greatest needs, unconditional love and acceptance. Jean Vanier said that "there is nothing in existence that can completely fulfill the needs of the human heart," and I am convinced that the love and acceptance that I crave and want and seek are not out somewhere in the world to be found (*Becoming Human* 7). Christians sometimes talk about the clichéd God-shaped hole in our hearts. I think that this could very well be true but I would add that I think we also have a people-shaped hole. If I was created for relationships with people, there has to be a permanent space for it and if I was created by a personal God then I have to have a permanent space for that. I don't think that the circumstances of life will ever allow both of these permanent spaces to be filled. Or, at least a part of me hopes that they wouldn't be as my former professor and now friend Rolf said to me, "Loneliness is an empty space but it is also an open space that invites." Loneliness becomes an open space to allow more of the life around me in. Without loneliness I would be oblivious to the connection I need and have around me. I need loneliness to remind me of the connections I have.

Loneliness is Nice but He is Not My Friend.

I will never be ashamed of feeling lonely but I will also not be content with a lingering and devouring loneliness because as beautiful as I mention it is, it is also very ugly. The ugly part of it scares me and I hate it. The ugly part has turned me into a horrible wreck at times. I was also quite annoyed to find out that it can have an effect on my health. "Loneliness not only alters behavior but shows up in measurements of stress hormones, immune function, and cardiovascular function. Over time, these changes in physiology are compounded in ways that may be hastening millions of people to an early grave" (Cacioppo and Patrick 5). This is frightening and it is also why loneliness can never be my friend.

I took a short professional questionnaire on loneliness the other day. I scored high for loneliness. I took it again and got the same result. I took it two days later and again the same result. This frustrates me because it tells me the most obvious fact that I am lonely but it also tells me that there is a piece of me convincing myself that I am not lonely. I can and will admit I am lonely but I would not say I would be on the high end. If I am lonely I can accept and embrace the beautiful things I get out of it but what if it lingers in a painful health-affecting despair? What if it does not go anywhere? I don't want an early grave like that quote says.

Let me talk about the horrible wreck piece that I mentioned. Loneliness can make me a horribly clingy and depressed person. It is almost as if I freak out and begin to grab onto anyone or anything that will make me feel whole and together. I get scared and fear rejection so I do everything I can to make myself appear better. I put on facades and find a plethora of social lies flowing from my mouth, "Let's do this again sometime," "I had a really good time," just so people will maybe let me in and I won't be lonely, all the while knowing I did not really enjoy their company. (I sense the rolling of eyes and the scoffing of dear friends that I have said this to. Put your conscience at ease. I do also use these statements as truths, as convoluted as that is to say, ha). Henri Nouwen writes that "[a]s long as our loneliness brings us together with the hope that together we no longer will be alone, we castigate each other with our unfilled and unrealistic desires for oneness, inner tranquility and the uninterrupted experience of communion" (30). I think he is right. It does me no good to pretend I enjoyed your company when I didn't and it does you no good either. I don't like becoming someone I am not, and in the process castigating and hurting the people around me, which ultimately leaves me lonelier. However, sometimes I feel that is all I have had the ability to do in the hardest and darkest part of my pain.

I am kind of scared of these two things I mention: The fact that loneliness can affect my long-term health and the way my behaviour can change. It contributes to my naturally anxious personality quite well. I have been frustrated because I can see something beautiful in loneliness that motivates me and connects me more with the people around me that I wish I could feel the pang of loneliness but avoid the negative consequences. I almost feel as though I am somehow being punished for being lonely. However, I do suppose that regardless of the beauty I see in loneliness, it is not something I like to feel. I have decided I will have a love-hate relationship with it. I will love the beautiful and hate the ugly. I will let it motivate me into new spaces but it will never be my friend. In the end, I do have the choice to stay lonely or make efforts to connect with those around me. I don't have to let loneliness affect my health. I also don't have to become that clingy person if I accept loneliness as simply a part of the human experience and trust that it will pass as I continue to open myself and dialogue honestly with the world around me.

Hmmm... Yep... I am a Loner

There is another part of me, however, the part that would be a hermit living on a beach somewhere in a tropical country with my own cult-like religion, eating locusts and honey. I have begun to call this part of me The Loner, which exudes the solitary and craves solitude. I never used to understand solitude. I was never taught it. I found it strange one day many years ago when my counselor challenged me by telling me she used to go out for dinner alone. She was a married woman and this did not make sense to me. It had never really crossed my mind why someone would willingly want to be on his or her own. At the same time, I breathed a sigh of relief because I knew I always wanted this. I remember as a child, growing up on an acreage, loving to go by myself on bike rides or wander into the bush alone. The challenge, and encouragement, she put forth set me on a journey into the very loner nature that I am. It was not long after that experience that I sought out being alone more and more. For a time Tim Hortons became my refuge. I would spend countless hours there, apart from everyone and everything familiar. I loved it, I still do. I have come to greatly seek out solitude and being alone. I have been reading a book written by Anneli Rufus called *Party of One: The Loner's Manifesto* and I am refreshed as she talks of being a loner as simply just another state of being. There is a huge part of me that is a loner and, all things considered, when you look at my life in its current entirety I can probably be identified as a loner.

Although, accepting this need for solitude, or identifying myself as a loner did not come as easily as that last paragraph may have made it sound. I had to overcome two obstacles in learning to love and seek out the solitude I wanted. The first one is that I had to enter fully into my loneliness and ask myself what it was. It was facing the fears and questions that I have been talking about in regards to loneliness thus far. In entering into the loneliness that I felt I found solitude because I realized that having someone around or not having someone around said nothing intrinsically about who I was or wasn't. Being alone and having solitude became just another state of being. A state in which allowed me to enter deeply into my very reflective and retrospective self. I found a huge piece of myself that I desired and needed in entering into loneliness. I love my alone time so much and loneliness has all the more place of importance in keeping me from as I mentioned earlier, becoming a hermit.

The second obstacle was guilt. I have felt and still do feel guilty at times when I am sitting at home doing my thing and I get asked if I would like to hang out with someone. I feel guilty because I really don't want to go out as I am having a great time at home alone but I do not want to hurt the person's feelings as they know I am just sitting at home alone. I also feel guilty at times when I am at home alone, enjoying myself, and I get the feeling I should call someone to hang out with me, not because I want to but because that is what I feel would be expected of me. And sometimes I have given into this guilt and it does not bode well because I can become quite ornery and be somewhat distant, remaining somewhat in my own little world. This is not respectful to myself or to the person that has given me the great gift of their time. I am learning that I need to really let go of this guilt and, if anything, let it be a signal to me to honor myself and honor the people around me. If I need to be alone, I need to be alone. It will not be respectful for me to be untrue to myself and spend time with someone when I do not want to spend time with someone.

In Anneli Rufus' book she states, in regards to friends, as self-professed loner, that "[w]e pick the cream of the crop, then expect them to understand that we want to be alone" (66). I believe this to be true. I am very picky with who I let remotely close. At the same time I think I need to communicate better to those friends I hold dear that I do need to be alone because I know I have hurt people by pushing them away out of my need to be alone. Something painfully funny to me is that I did have a friend that understood this more than anyone has in my life because he himself was a loner of sorts. I wish I had recognized this before I myself ironically questioned a distance that was growing between us, on his part. I expected him to be like the societal norm non-loner and so I made attempts to put more of my non-loner foot forward, and it is out of this non-loner that I pushed him away. I miss this friendship because it allowed me a very relaxed freedom to be alone if I wanted and never be questioned. I wish I had given the same respect, as "[b]eing friends with a loner requires patience and the wisdom that distance does not mean dislike" (Rufus 71). I knew this.

So, I am loner. I am unsure how to fully define what being a loner means. It is not that I despise having people in my life because I know that I need them, and want them, it is just that I want people to give me space. To quote Rufus again, she writes, "FOR LONERS, FRIENDS are all the more essential because in many cases they are our sole conduits to the outside world. They are channels, filters, valves, rivers from the outback to the sea. When we find good ones, we pour ourselves into them" (Rufus 73). I am not one to keep a lot of close friends. I let very few close but those I do I let in are very close. And once they are close come hell or high water I am committed to them. One or two, maybe three, is more than enough. I also am quite aware that I instantly attempt to distance myself from anything that would tie me or connect me to a larger group. I feel as though I am smothered and I lose a piece of myself when I become known as being a part of a larger group. I cringe at being asked to be part of a group. I would rather eat dirt at times than to be part of a group. I know that there is a need for humans to belong to community, the feeling of loneliness tells me so, but there is another huge part of me that hates it. Jean Vanier writes about this paradox quite nicely saying that "as humans we are caught between competing drives, the drive to belong, to fit in and be a part of something bigger than ourselves, and the drive to let our deepest selves rise up, to walk alone, to refuse the accepted and comfortable, and this can mean, at least for a time, the acceptance of anguish" (*Becoming Human* 18).

I don't want to be lost in the masses. I am a very weird person, I have been told, just yesterday called an odd-ball. I think it's because I do not let myself fully enter into the masses. I stay on the fringe of most groups or all groups. Groups seem to have this tendency of forming so tightly on similarities that we lose our differences and it is in our differences that so much can be gained. It is a good thing that people join together to have a stronger collective voice but it is a bad thing when the individuals within those groups lose or sacrifice their individuality based on the collective thought. People can be lost or excluded from the group based on the fact that they don't exactly fit the mold. In doing so, important voices are lost. When exclusion happens, groups become both stagnant and so set in their belief system that they begin to subjugate any thought contrary to their own. In fact they have to subjugate in order to protect the security of the group and the security of themselves within the group.

> Human relationships are essentially those of alienated automatons, each basing his security on staying close to the herd, and not being different in thought, feeling or action. While everybody tries to be close as possible to the rest, everybody remains utterly alone, pervaded by the deep sense of insecurity, anxiety and guilt which always results when human separateness cannot be overcome. (Fromm 78)

Sadly, driven by the fear of being alone or separate, we form tightly knit groups that have the danger of alienating and excluding important elements of the world, even elements that are silenced but ever-present within individuals of a tight knit group. On a small scale this appears in the very smart, but shy, grade-schooler who is excluded based on his shyness. His smartness is missed because all that the other children can see is his shyness and so they subjugate out of protection. On a greater scale, the impact of this subjugation and alienation has played out in painfully destructive moments in history; it screams of the Crusades, the treachery of the holocaust, and the despicable genocide in Rwanda, to name a few.

I am scared of this, and of losing my individuality, and so I avoid being tightly tied to groups. I do not want to alienate and I do not want to be alienated. I want to be an individual and I want to be acknowledged as individual. I never want that to be lost or confused or identified simply based on being a part of some community or organization.

I suppose that me joining the local curling club (I don't curl, not sure why this example has come to mind) will more than likely not end up in some horrific genocide, so I know there is another piece of this to be said. I must admit that in joining a group there is a part of me that fears rejection. I tell myself that I do not need to belong to something to be important, which is true, but it also goes against a piece of how I came to be created and evolved within community. I tell myself that I will do it on my own. I hate admitting this because I don't want to change this piece of myself, fear of rejection or not. Enter pride and arrogance. I am certain that I have convinced myself that I can do this alone and I will show you and

big will the loss be? Who is going to fill the void left by
my newly married friend? It also confirms yet again the
fact that I have chosen this lonely life and it makes me
wonder if I am right in choosing it.

But let me say this to married friends before I
inappropriately and unintentionally spread on some sort
of thick guilt. I know for a fact that I would be quite
disappointed in you if you didn't put a huge amount of
time and commitment into your marriage. You need to
put the effort into your most important relationship and
sometimes that does mean that us single folk have to
allow you the space to do so. At the same time, I would
say to not forget about us single folk as the reality is that
you may be our most important relationship. To me, this
has meant knowing that you, my married friends, don't
value me any less when you have less time for me or
when you aren't always able to talk when I need to talk.
It has also meant acknowledging and fully realizing the
freedom of my singleness and offering it as a gift to you. I
can be the one to bend and adjust my schedule in order
to spend time with you because my schedule does not
have to take into account a wife and kids, so I can be the
one to flex, be the one to make the trip to see you, or
meet you three quarters of the way instead of in the
middle.

And then I also realize that married people are also
not completely immune to this pain of living alone and
single. I was talking with my married friend Mike about
this current topic and he identified with me within the
context of marriage. Mike and his wife Amy came to an
understanding and realization that their relationship was
not a cure or fix for their feelings of aloneness, and
loneliness at times. Despite being married, they could not

always be there for each other and they could not always understand each other, or fully agree with each other. Ultimately, they could not live inside one another's heads. I find this strangely reassuring because it tells me that even within the closest human relationships there is a feeling of aloneness and of separateness that is simply part of the human experience. Loneliness is an inescapable reality. If feeling separate and alone is simply a part of the plethora of human experiences, then it is simply okay that at times I feel alone and that no one understands me because no one, save the one who made me, ever fully will.

We are all alone as much as we are separate beings with separate thoughts, feelings, opinions, etc. Part of this inescapable existence is embracing and truly enjoying who we are. In my aloneness and solitude I have learned to have the greatest time, full of inside jokes shared between my Creator and me, as I have continually embraced all the insecurity, the strength, the broken, and the collected, parts of myself. When I am alone, I am simply me and it is beautiful. There is a freedom in knowing that I am not subconsciously worrying and responding to those around me in order to fit societal polities and norms. When I am alone, I can enter into the eccentric parts of myself that no one, except for the one who created me, would understand or take simply at face value. Take, for example, how I like to talk in weird voices to myself when I am alone, or how I act or pretend to be someone else almost like you would play house when you were younger. I would not be embarrassed to share these moments with the people close to me but there is something about those moments that I enjoy having as just mine. Sometimes I don't want people to think I am funny, or weird, or nice, or enjoyable, or odd, or crazy, or fun to be around. I don't want a laugh, a cry, a smile, smirk, or a pat on the back. Sometimes I just want to be exactly who I am with no thoughts about it, just to be, just to exist, to be exactly who I am created to be, like a wild animal free to roam. The only place I have found that I can do this in entirety is when I am alone.

Ignorance can be bliss. I have talked about how we are all alone, married or not, and how there is much to be found and expressed in being alone. I have left out the other piece where I say as much as I rationalize this life alone, there needs to be life together and I cannot simply rely on the thought that we are all alone at times to get me through. I have had to learn to be quite intentional in staying connected with the people around me. It has meant facing the difficult task of reevaluating friendships and restructuring them as friends' marriages and families come into the picture. It has meant letting go of friendships at times, leaving a very large hole and void waiting to be filled. Enter the pang of loneliness that devours my contentedness but draws me closer and invites me into what Michael Bernard Fitzgerald's lyrics suggest, brand new spaces in brand new faces. Living alone can be a choice as much as being married is, both have their relational obstacles.

7

Who Is The Idiot?

Here is a fictional character in a fictional, but very reflective of reality, story you will all like.

You should have seen him. He was of the likes of www.peopleofwalmart.com, a complete loser. So, I was standing behind him in the line at the local grocery store, in the Express Line. We all know that the Express Line clearly says, "15 items or less." He had at least 20 items. I know because I counted before he even got to the front of the line. What was he thinking? He was clearly over the 15 item limit. Sure enough he gets to the front of the line and the girl working the cash register says, "Sir, this is the Express Line."

Quite boggled, the idiot says, "Sorry, the what line?" as he precedes to unload his soon-to-be purchases onto the conveyor belt. Like, come on buddy! Are ya new?

"The Express Line, Sir! I am sorry, you will have to go to another register as this is Express Line only!" came the voice from the now agitated girl behind the cash register.

"What? Ohhh, goodness, I'm sorry," came his reply as he packed up his over the limit groceries back into the cart. We all scoffed and rolled our eyes as he pushed his cart back through line of people to find another till. Oh, the characters that come out of grocery stores.

What an idiot! Come on! How thick do you have to be? People are so stupid! On a more serious note, where do these people come from? Really! Seriously, where do they come from? They are never my friends; they are certainly never my friend's friends, my parents, my siblings, my aunts, my uncles, or my cousins either. At the very least, the ones I like anyway. Who are these idiots?

This question had me quite puzzled for awhile because I thought it odd to simply chalk it up to the assuming statement we have all used or, at the very least, thought, "People are so stupid." I am people. My friends are people. The people I keep close to me are people. If I use the endearing and sweeping statement that "boy, oh boy, people sure are stupid," I have to be willing to lump myself, and all those I love, into this generalization as well. I am not stupid nor am I an idiot. I also don't think those I love are either. At least I like thinking so. I am patting myself on the back right now. This patting on the back is contrary to the thought that me or my people are stupid.

Both of these seeming truths cannot be right. So, this is the way I see it. I am either an idiot, or not an idiot, along with the entirety of humanity. My pride and arrogance calls me to humbly admit that I choose the truth that I am an idiot along with the entirety of humanity because I have seen some real idiots out there and I am not willing to let this insult to go unwarranted, even at the cost of the exposure of my own idiocy. I can be a real idiot at times. Just the other day I walked into one of those automatic doors that are supposed to open when you walk up to them and then waited a few seconds in hopes that it would still open. It didn't. Forgive me for missing the sign that mentioned it was broken. Yes, it was funny, and yes, I was kind of an idiot. Is this idiocy any worse than the guy who mistook the express lane in the grocery store for a normal lane? I am sure that there is some website somewhere that rates these sorts of things but in my superior expertise in weighing the idiocy of events, I would say no. So why is it that too often I forget that I am a part of the idiocy and stupidity that make up common humanity?

Pride and arrogance constantly lurk in every corner of my life, waiting to subtly implant themselves within every crack and crevice of my being, telling me that I am better, I am smarter, I am nicer, and doggone it people like me! Pride craftily and constantly looms. I do something nice for someone, crack a good joke, or write something clever and it makes me smile. I think the smile is good because it connects me with the good things in life but sometimes the smile turns into a subtle, "Well… hmmmm… that was a nice thing for me to do! How nice am I? Very nice actually! Who else would do that? I bet pretty much no one! Why aren't people as nice as me? Other people should be as nice as me! I don't know anyone nicer!"

Well, pat me on the back and give me a trophy or a nobel peace prize because heavens to Betsy I have the ability to be nice! Did I forget that I once was labeled a complainer, which is somewhat true, or that I have been known to gossip, or that I am horribly good at interrupting other people's conversations? These are not the nicest things to do but they are quite minor right? ... Right?

I read a book on Snobbery, *Snobbery: The American Version*. It made me quite aware of the fact that there are many facets of snobbery, the looking down of noses at those appearing to be below. Joseph Epstein quite cleverly and humorously presents snobbery about everything from food and fashion, to politics and social status. What became more apparent is that we can all be full of snobbery. "Even caring a great deal for someone does not lessen the need most of us to feel to think ourselves oh just a touch better: smarter or wittier or more commonsensical or better looking or larger-hearted or subtler, better adjusted, more logical – pick any three, and add a few items of your own invention not listed here" (Epstein 241). I know this is what I do. I pick my one, two, or three things and then somehow use them to levy myself above the idiots around me, all the while forgetting that even if these things I use to levy myself are my strengths, I have a whole whack of other characteristics and things about me that are horribly wretched. And some of you fine readers may be thinking, "Ohhh, I am not snobby." What about holding yourself higher because you think you are above or better than the act of snobbery, being snobby about not being a snob and holding your nose in the air at those that are snobs in the traditional sense. I also do this and I am quite well at it, I think.

The Biblical book of Romans offers some practical advice when Paul writes about everyone falling short of the glory of God (Romans 3:23). When I choose to look down on the idiot in front of me in the line at the local grocery store, who do I think I am? Even if I was smarter, wiser, less of an idiot than that man, and there is no way to know, what would it matter in the broad perspective that no one can match the glory of God, perfection. It would be like the idiot at the grocery store and I trying to reach the stars with a ladder; he with a 10ft ladder, me with a 15ft ladder. Does the extra 5ft matter when we would both still have a million bijillion feet to climb?

The same question that Joseph Epstein asks himself within the pages of his book echoes greatly in my own pondering, "…Why do I still find it necessary to look down on some people? What do I have to prove?" I try my darndest at times not to do this but nevertheless, I catch myself in one way or another subtly one-upping another in my mind and less often, but more disgustingly, outwardly. Snobbery gets in the way of relationships. It somehow convinces me to label others as unworthy, no good, infantile, immature, stupid, or ignorant without me even noticing. I end up dismissing people like I were picking fruit at the grocery store; poking and prodding until I can find something that I find distasteful. I miss the fullness and greatness that I believe people are meant and created to be based on a few quick perceptions.

I let myself enter the delusion that I somehow have the bird's eye view of life, making my poking and prodding quite justified. Within my mind, I throw out my life credentials, the things I have done, the things I have experienced, the things I know, the education I have, or the conversations I have had as if they are the full blown gospel truth, the be all and end all of life. I use them like a God-given gift to filter any thought, action, or statement that anyone gives me. I will be able to tell you how right, how wrong, or how eye rolling it is. I would be quite proud of this gift, who wouldn't, if only it were true.

Psychologists use a term called selective exposure to describe, among other situations, our mind's ability to pay closer attention to self-praise than criticism. We protect our self-image to the point of being able to ignore or block out all negative information, as true as it may be, about ourselves. "To put it simply in order to build or defend our self-esteem, we tell ourselves lies about how we perceive our experience. Without fully realizing it, we interpret what happens to us in ways that are comforting, flattering, or both" (Feldman 132). If this is true, then I have to admit that my God-given gift is not true. Sadly, and fortunately for you, I will admit that I do not have the right to roll my eyes at you or your friends for the stupidity that you for surely exhibit. There is absolutely nothing that I have done, experienced, or learned, or will ever do, experience, or learn that will ever give me the upper hand of superiority that my inferior self-esteem and confidence crave.

The feeling of inferiority is something that at one time or another we have all experienced. There is always someone bigger, better, or smarter. There is always someone higher on the social ladder. This is far from profound and we have all heard it since we were knee-high to a grasshopper but sometimes there is a deep need, or desire, within me that cries out, "I have something to offer, please don't just glaze over me." And the reality is that sometimes, despite my best attempts to simply be myself, I have often felt glazed over and ignored. And when this happens, snobbery comes in quite handy. I get to hold my head high in whatever area I feel I have an advantage and snub the rest of you idiots who first snubbed me. Then, in turn, we all snub each other on some level creating a disconnected society, whereby we all miss the real and genuine people we all probably, and actually, are.

There is another side of snobbery. Sometimes the things that people are snobby or at least seem snobby about are quite splendid. I say this because I know that sometimes the things that I am snobby about are actually quite enjoyable and I hold them up as if no one, or very few, would understand or fathom how great they are. Take drinking wine, for example. I like wine. I like wine a lot. As I have entered further and further into wine culture I will admit I have become more and more of a wine snob. I had roommate a short while back that would drink his wine out of the first glass that he saw in the cupboard, despite the fact that there was a whole shelf in the cupboard devoted to wine glasses. Can you believe it? Drinking wine out a glass meant for milk, juice, or pop? Come on! I say this sarcastically and jokingly but I really had a snobbishly hard time with it and I would internally scoff and roll my eyes every time I saw this despicable display. And yes, this is worthy of a, "Get over yourself Dustin." However, this is what I would like to share about this event. There is something I have found quite delightful and enjoyable in holding a wine glass in my hand. It is almost as if the shape and feeling of its glassy wonderfulness, its long slender stem and large spacious, inviting top, in my hand transports me to another time and another place. I could be in France celebrating the 50th birthday of a local dignitary. Not that I would ever want to but I could be. This is the magic allure that a wine glass holds for me, that and the glorious bounty of fermented liquid grapeness. I say all of this because there is more to snobbery than simply feeling inferior or wanting to prove oneself. I believe that sometimes there is something valuable or important, or magical, hidden behind people's snobbery. The hidden part becomes the problem because at the heart of snobbery is the thought, "I have something you don't." I should not look down on my former roommate for not seeing, or understanding, the same brilliance I see in how magical a wine glass can be because I have never offered that thought to him.

I have decided that there are two responses I need to have in regards to my arrogance. First, I need to realize that snobbery says something about how I view myself. Through my snobbery, I am either attempting to prove my value and worth, or holding my nose in the air in spite because I have felt jilted. I know that I do not want to be or come off as an arrogant snob but that sometimes I do. If I accept that part of me is simply trying to prove myself, I can allow myself enough grace to acknowledge this arrogance and snobbery long enough to challenge it. In the same sentence, I need to say that the same grace then needs to extend to the rest of you fine folk out there. If you are snobby, or when you are snobby, I need to be able to simply smile and recognize that maybe you just need to be acknowledged. Or maybe that at some point in your life you were so starved for acknowledgment that your only defense is to currently hold your nose in the air. If this is the case, I would hope that I should be able to love you all the more.

Second, whether or not snobbery is simply an illusion of grandeur personally installed in my life to give me an ego boost, it should not stop there. I think I should be asking myself the question, "Other than an ego boost, what is it I get from the areas in my life that I am arrogantly snobby?" I am convinced that in the same way I find magic in a wine glass, I can also find treasures like honesty, genuineness, or honor somewhere in the other things I hold my nose in the air about. Once I identify the treasures within my snobbery, I think that I then need to somehow offer them as gifts to those around me, instead of hidden snubs, sneers, or scoffs. I should be offering the magic of wine glasses to my old roommate instead of internally scoffing. The reality is that the things I can be snobby about are not really mine to own anyway. How do I think that I can own the magic allure of a wine glass? A wine glass is an ageless piece of glassware that has its roots in ancient civilization. I can't own that. Or take, for example, the snobbery of not being snobby. How could I own the virtue of kindness or genuineness? It is meant to be shared and besides, the minute I think I have complete kindness or genuineness in my grasp is the same minute it diminishes in my hand as if I were holding a melting ice cube.

However, if I grasp onto the idea that the objects of my snobbery are not mine to own, I have less to be snobby about. And when I am snobby I can catch and challenge myself to think of ways to offer the objects of my snobbery as gifts to those around me. In the same way when I sense an air of snobbery from you, I can creatively think about ways that I can open up a dialogue so that you will share your gifts of snobbery with me.

Take this as an example. Accomplishments can easily become areas of snobbery. I can become quite proud and arrogant about the things I have done and accomplished.

It makes sense that I would become snobby about such things because accomplishment is pretty awesome and it speaks volumes about who we are created and meant to be. However, it is not mine to own because you also have accomplishments and things in your life to be proud of. You also have overcome obstacles and challenges, all of which I have not experienced, in at least the way you have experienced them. How does one measure and compare accomplishments... the amount of praise one receives or the amount of monetary value one receives? What then of personal and private accomplishments like overcoming an addiction? I am not sure that there is a proper measurement bar out there to evaluate and compare how great I am, or you are, in comparison to everyone else. Therefore, I think that my accomplishments, and the things I am proud of, cannot ever be something to hold my nose in the air about. They simply become a general statement about our human ability and capability to accomplish and become what is offered to us all. Instead of snubbing my nose at those around me, that have seemingly and apparently not accomplished what I have, there is an opportunity to have a dialogue about hopes, dreams, and the obstacles that all of us have in the way.

Joseph Epstein concludes his book on snobbery with the thought that "[s]nobbery will die on the day when none of us needs reassurance of his worth, when society is so well balanced as to eliminate every variety of injustice, when fairness rules, and kindness and generosity, courage and honor are all rightly, revered" (251). I will admit that I am a bit of an idealist at times but I am not sure I could ever internalize and live what this quote implies. Part of me wants to try though because I do not want the snobbery that is infesting and infecting me, as well as the world around me, to continue to impact even the most distant of my relationships. So, until the day when snobbery dies, I will settle on the thought that we are all idiots, each and every one of us, especially me.

8

Thinking Outside the Box

One of the biggest pains is the feeling of being misunderstood. In being misunderstood, all that I am seems to be lost, diminished, and handicapped. I feel like a flattened character in a cheap Harlequin romance novel. I try my hardest, in fact I try too hard to be understood, and yet sometimes the inevitable happens. I am misunderstood. When the inevitable does happen, when I am known for something I am not, I somehow think that if I talk loud enough or long enough the walls of misunderstanding will crumble and I will be heard. I don't think that this has proven true because my voice is croaky and sore.

I have decided, quite assuredly, that I am a strange individual and have even been labeled as such. I have learned to be okay with this or at the very least have attempted to take comfort in the fact that some of the most strange or crazy out there have also turned out to be the most brilliant, like Einstein with his wild hair or Van Gogh who cut his own ear off. While I don't imagine cutting my own ear off would be pleasant, or even in the realm of my strangeness, I have always felt as if I were on the very fringe of the societal norm. I feel like my mind operates on a completely different wavelength. I am unsure if it is simply the norm to feel completely unique but a lot of the time I feel like I am on a completely different page than everyone else.

This would be okay apart from the pain. To be and feel misunderstood is to feel and be unknown, and to be unknown is a very lonely place to be. It causes me to draw into myself, shutting the world out that seemingly doesn't get me anyway. I take my eccentricities and go curl up in a ball of seclusion. It's comfortable and it's safe but as I stated it can also be lonely. Other times I think that I can quite easily put on the mask of social connectedness and of normality and truly enjoy myself, putting aside or ignoring my feelings of being misunderstood.

Then again, we are all different, unique, and are filled with our own eccentricities. Maybe I am not as strange as I think but who has an accurate measure anyway? I must be willing to admit that the same way I am misunderstood is the same way I misunderstand others. I make assumptions about everyone else, placing them neatly in a well-wrapped box. I sometimes even tie the bow of self-righteousness on top because I know that my assumptions are for surely accurate. I am sure that most times I probably fall into the category of making an ass out of you and me, as the stupid adage about making assumptions states.

I suppose I have to eat my own words in writing this because just the other day amidst a conflict, I said to a co-worker, "Why do you think you know who I am?"

His response was quite clever, "Well, why do you think you know me?"

"I don't but I don't pretend to," was my somewhat self-righteous and one-upping response.

This is what I am learning. To be misunderstood is to be human, as much as being my own separate entity with my own separate mind filled with my own separate thoughts, opinions, or experiences keeps me from knowing another individual in complete entirety. Until I have the ability to walk a mile in another's shoes, and also walk a mile in their brain, misunderstanding will always be a part of my human experience. And I would love to be able to do this but "we can't – no more than we can tell whether the yellow experience we have when we look at a school bus is the same yellow experience that others have when they look at the same school bus" (Gilbert 42). The reality is that the only way I can understand another is through my own subjective experience. I base every thought, opinion, and experience that another individual shares with me on every thought, opinion and experience that I have had. Sadly there is no such thing as a true objective and unbiased view of another.

> [O]ur beliefs about the reasons others do what they do have more to do with our own subjective experience of their behavior and how it impacts us. How we assess them depends on whether we feel good or bad in response to their actions. That is the nature of subjectivity. Then we react

> to what we imagine they are doing 'to us' (or to
> others), and they then react, in the same way, to
> our reactions. (Richardson 37)

And a cycle of biased and unfair opinions and thoughts of
one another begins. At best, I completely miss some of
the great and wonderful people around me; at worst, I
create an arrogant and ignorant wall that pushes the
other into a rigid box where anything said or done will
only confirm the rigidity of the box. If I have decided that
you are a complainer everything you say from then on will
only confirm to me that you are a complainer because I
can selectively choose what I want to hear. Simon and
Garfunkel have a line in their song "The Boxer" that goes
like this, "A man hears what he wants to hear and
disregards the rest."

> While we're often curious and engaged by the
> world, we're also careful with how we spend our
> mental energy. For instance, when we walk down
> the street, we don't examine every crack in the
> sidewalk, every car on the road, the face of every
> person we pass, the shape of each cloud in the
> sky, the path of every bird. First of all, we'd never
> make it to the corner. But also, we simply don't
> have the cognitive capacity to consciously
> consider every aspect of what we encounter. We
> pay attention to a few things and don't spend
> much time thinking about the rest. (Feldman 47)

Mental capacity or not, I don't like to think that I
would treat another human being as I would a crack in
the sidewalk, simply not worth the time to think about.
But yet, to some extent my limited human mind demands
me to package and box people in this same way because

it can't function otherwise. I just need to keep myself aware of the fact that there is not a box big enough to capture the smallest of brains, with all of its experiences, thoughts, and opinions. Any label or thought, positive or negative, that I have toward another is limited. The thought of another being arrogant could also be informed by the thought that that individual may feel inferior, which could be further informed by the fact that they may have a past experience of abuse or neglect. It would be somewhat unfair of me to simply put them in a rigid box of arrogance based on a surface level evaluation.

People are mysterious beyond what my conscious mind can process at any given moment. There is no way to comprehend in one thought, or even a million thoughts, the breadth, the width, and depth of one's mind, heart, and soul. The best I can do is to as loosely as possible construct the assumptions my mind is bound to make and allow the boxes that I place people in the ability to easily crumble. If I have the constant ability to learn more about myself, how can I ever think that I would have the ability to peg another down? I can't and won't. Instead I will enter into one of greatest things about relationship, the unknown. There is always something more I can know about another and if I remain with as few conclusions or assumptions about who they are I will forever remain intrigued. Every new story, experience, thought, or opinion that is shared becomes just one more aspect of the never-ending beauty that makes up an individual. I should marvel in the delight of a broadened view of another and never be shocked that how I saw them to be is not who they are in actuality.

Ultimately, it boggles my mind that, considering all of this reflecting, I have the ability to understand anyone at all. The truth is that maybe I don't have the ability to understand anyone and all I have is the invitation or pursuit of understanding. In this light, relationship becomes the pursuit of knowing and understanding, entering into what I have described above as the unknown.

Entering the unknown is somewhat frightening to me because anything can happen. If I can neatly package and label everyone around me into some sort of category, then I know what to expect and I can seemingly control the world around me. Maybe the more scary part is how the human mind has the ability to do this so cleverly. We gather information based on a few experiences and then apply that information to the general whole, just as I would assume that all cracks in the sidewalk are the same. A jock is a jock and when I meet someone who strikes me as a jock, I can selectively choose and pick out the information that he/she shares to confirm my belief. And once I have decided that this new friend is a jock, it is easier for me to simply allow this belief to remain than to challenge it.

I can gain control of my world by labeling and making assumptions about the people around me. The more and better I package people, the less I have to be challenged by. I can put the jock in the jock box and never allow myself to experience their intellect because jocks stereotypically don't have much to offer intellectually. I can label you as arrogant and write you off instead of confronting the pain of rejection I feel, which could inadvertently have nothing to do with you. Or I can label you as arrogant and pompous instead of acknowledging the pain and hurt I may have caused you. I am sorry. I can remain whole, together, and complete if I can hide behind the labels and boxes I put you in because echoed in this way of thinking is the thought that I have everything about life around me figured out. I can be an expert about life around me, smart, opinionated, and wise, never allowing myself to be truly challenged.

I want to return to the label that I gave myself at the beginning of this chapter, misunderstood. I can identify myself as misunderstood but at the same time I suppose that I am labeling you as ignorant. If I am misunderstood, you must be ignorant of who I am. I am unsure if it is fair to label you as ignorant without giving you at least a chance to know me. If I am as strange, different, and misunderstood as I have convinced myself that I am, I need to do my best to be heard and understood. In doing so, I will confirm one of three things. One, that I am indeed strange and different, and you aren't ignorant; two, that I am not strange and different, and you are not ignorant; or three, which I think would be highly unlikely, that you actually are ignorant. If I feel greatly misunderstood, it is my responsibility to express myself and speak up to those important to me, instead of labeling them as ignorant. One such expression is how I have picked up creating and doing art. It allows me to express a part of my very abstract brain to those around me. To those who are not close to me, or that do not matter, and I need to be wise enough to know the difference, I need to embrace the thought that it is none of my business what other people think of me.

And so, I will take misunderstanding, as misunderstanding is, as an invitation to know and be known. With every feeling of misunderstanding, there is assumption that could be challenged. And with every assumption to be challenged, there is a truth about love, life, and relationship.

9

Never Cry Wolf

We all know the story of the boy who cried wolf. The nice shepherd boy bored with his job of watching sheep attempts to rudely entertain himself by crying wolf, stirring up the townsfolk into the pitchfork mob anger that having a wolf after your sheep usually deserves. However, there is no wolf after the sheep and the boy gets a good chuckle out of the fact that he fooled everyone. Slightly perturbed the townsfolk go back to doing what townsfolk do. The boy cries, "Wolf," again. Again, setting off the townsfolk, again getting a chuckle leaving the townspeople even more perturbed. Then the inevitable happens. A wolf actually does come after sheep. This time he cries, "Wolf!" and no one comes. Losing all the trust and credibility that he had as faithful shepherd he had no one to come to his aid.

I remind you of this timeless childhood story because I would like to tell you about something affecting me and my relationships. It's called NCWD, Never Cry Wolf Disease. This horrible syndrome attacks the very fabric of my relationships, and many of the relationships around me. In early onset, NCWD is a mere annoyance but as it progresses it can have severe impact on levels of trust and credibility, possibly crippling or even ruining relationship. At its best, NCWD will simply become something that hinders relationship and at its worst, it can tear through the micro-fibers of trust that bind relationships together.

At its core, NCWD is, for lack of better words, a lack of commitment to others. One of my greatest friends very early on in our friendship had temporarily lost all credibility and trust from me because 5 of the first 6 times we ever planned to hang out he bailed. I am not sure how we managed to become as good of friends as we are now but it did take awhile for the trust to be rebuilt and for him to gain back his credibility. This is a classic case of NCWD because amidst that 5 out of 6 bails, and even long after, I expected that he would bail on me. I would make plans but just like the townsfolk did, I never really believed him. I took on the I will believe it when I see it attitude. If we planned to go for coffee, I would come with books or work to do, or I would always ensure I had a back-up plan. He was crying wolf and I was calling bullshit.

I wish this was the only example of NCWD that I have experienced. I see it everywhere and I watch it happen to others, and I do it to others. I have made a plan and then for the embarrassing and shameful reason that something better came up, I have bailed with some lame excuse. I get a violent disgust that rattles through my body as I think of the disrespect of this act. And yet, I think that there are more people than just I that do this. Or maybe, more tactfully, we won't commit to an invitation until we are sure nothing else more exciting is going on; "Ohhh, I am not sure what is going on Friday night yet, I will let you know."

I feel there is a plague of NCWD moving through my generation. I had a family friend who I consider to be my Aunt once say to me, "What is with you younger people not being able to commit to anything?" I think she is right. I feel that in my mere thirty years that I have noticed less and less commitment in the people around me. I am unsure why exactly this seems to be true, maybe it's North American individualism at its best but, regardless, I think it has lasting effects other than a few friends getting ditched once and awhile.

It comes down to not being able to trust a friend with the big important things in life if they are not willing to commit to the small things. How can I expect someone to trust me with details of his or her life if they can't even trust me to show up for a cup of coffee? I want my friends to know that I am there for them and that they are valuable to me. Bailing last minute with a lame excuse or canceling for better plans says more about the value I place on myself than it does about the value I place on the friendship. It also has the unfortunate ability to communicate to my friends that I am in the friendship solely for myself. A friendship is also about caring for and giving back to.

There is also a deeper element to this issue. If I continually allow myself to be a victim of NCWD, I will continually allow a distance to be created in my relationships. If I continually show a lack of commitment, it will eventually be returned with a lack of commitment from my friends. When this happens, the closeness that a friendship can be is lost. It is difficult to build a strong friendship on shifting sands.

Ultimately, sometimes I feel unsure about how much I can, or should, trust my friends. Assuredly, there is past hurt and a fear of being hurt again that keeps me from trusting at times. At the same time, I know that the vibe I get from the society or culture around me is that we are all in this alone. "Loyalty. Devotion. Those are haunting words from an older era, largely lost from our vocabulary" (McGinnis 174). I don't think that it has ever really been modeled to me what commitment in a friendship looks like. To me, commitment means an ever-growing and ever-changing relationship that never stagnates and never stops getting deeper. It means sticking through the hard times and learning to work through each other's faults, weaknesses, and arrogance.

However, I suppose that commitment is not easy because it exposes me to two horrible things, my friends and myself. As I stay committed to my friends, loyal and devoted, the more of them I am exposed to. This means seeing not only the nice things about my friends, all the stuff I love, but I begin to see their shit as well. There is something utterly unattractive about brokenness that makes me want to flee. At first glance, it would appear that I do not want to be friends with broken people, which is true, but the more true fact is that when I begin to see others' brokenness, their shit, it begins to remind me of my own shit that I like to avoid on the best of days. To see the arrogance or selfishness in another is simply a mirror reflecting back at me. Sometimes it has been easier to jump ship, labeling my friend as arrogant, ignorant, or selfish, than it is to stick it out and admit my own arrogance, ignorance, or selfishness.

I want friendships strong enough to last and endure the pain of hard times. I want my friends to know that I will always have their back and to know they have my back as well. I want to be able to share deeply what is affecting me and my world. I want to be able to share fears, dreams, and hopes. And I want to be able to do this with friends that I know will still be there when his or her phone rings with something better to do.

Friendships are not careless or haphazard. They are an intentional, beautiful, and life-giving responsibility. They require commitment and responsibility. Just as the poor little shepherd boy who cried wolf learned, that to be taken seriously you have to treat others responsibly, with respect, consistently. I cannot expect my friends to be there for me if I am not there for them. So, I promise you, my friends, that I will do my darndest to fight for a cure to NCWD, because you are worth it.

10

Dear Aunt Grace

Every time the word grace is mentioned I cannot help but think of my kind-hearted Aunt Grace. Growing up, her name never made any sense to me as it always seemed somewhat strange. It could be because I never knew what the word grace meant for the longest time, maybe even that it was a word. Regardless, I wondered why my grandparents chose such a name. Oddly enough when the word grace came into my vocabulary, it also did not make sense because grace was simply the name of my aunt. It would be like instead of using the word Ignorance, you would use Dustin. Hmmm … "Dustin is bliss." I could get used to that. This is similar to a possible vague recollection of an old story told about my aunt quite enjoying the song "Amazing Grace" when she was a child. I can't see why anyone in the right mind wouldn't adore a song labeling them as amazing. Upon growing a brain, the word grace and its meaning became more and more apparent to me. The beauty, the elegance, the goodness, and the love that this one word encapsulates tell me that my grandparents were no fools to use it as my aunt's namesake. What better way to honor a little bundle of joy and blessing than to name a child Grace.

As I reflect on the word grace and all that it can mean, and has meant in my life, there are a couple of examples that come to mind. There was the one time as a child that I drove our lawn tractor into the door of our truck. I expected a ton of fury and a hammer of punishment; instead all I got was some initial anger and frustration followed by complete absolution. There was another time when I was in my post-secondary education; taking the most challenging class I had ever taken, Advanced Theological Prolegomena. The very fact that I did not know what the very title of the class meant should have been a dead giveaway for how challenging it would be. The class also happened to be very small, four people, out of which I struggled the most, especially after one of the four dropped out. I was to present a research paper, an assignment I hadn't a clue about what I was doing. When it came my time to present I did the best I could but it became apparent quite quickly from the blank stares of the professor and the two others in the class that I clearly did not know what I was doing or maybe even saying. When I finished my blabbering, I got one of the kindest smiles and thank-yous from the professor that I have ever received. When I received my mark on the research paper, I found that I got an A- with the comments somewhere along the lines of, "This is not what I was looking for in the assignment but I appreciate the effort you put in." Grace.

Both of the above examples highlight something for me that I would like to be added to my friendship wish list, if there was or is such a thing. In regards to slamming a tractor into a truck, I think that I would like a lot of freedom to make mistakes in a friendship. In regards to my horrible assignment, I think that I would like the freedom to not be complete and together in my friendships. I want to talk more about these.

Gracefully Slamming a Tractor into a Truck

When I slammed the tractor into the truck I really did not mean to do so. In all honesty, I did know that I was headed right for it and at a considerable speed that would cause damage. However, I did not take into account our tractor's great ability to slow down and stop at the slowest speed known to man. I did use the brake thinking that I would stop before I would come close to hitting the truck. This did not happen. I made a mistake. The grace that I received from my parents in not being punished communicated two things. Firstly, that my remorse and guilt for the incident was punishment enough. More importantly, however, is the ability to make a mistake without it being held as a statement about who I was. The fact that I made a mistake had no impact about who I was as a person; it simply said that I was human. I suppose that this may not be the most profound thought but why is it that I catch myself writing people off at times, based on one or two unappealing actions?

I have been known to make one or two mistakes relationally. Surprisingly, one of the two was just today when I found out that I missed a friend's birthday celebration, which I promised I would be at. I am currently out at my grandparent's cabin where there is no cell coverage. I have been here for a week. I entered into the civilization of cell coverage for a few minutes today and found a few texts and a voicemail, both of disappointment and concern. I made a mistake and I am hoping for grace. I did not mean to miss the birthday that I said I would be at. In all reality, there are probably some things I could have done to ensure that I did not miss it. I could have made sure I knew the date instead of assuming it was later in the month. I could have given my friend a number where I could be reached at while I was gone. I could have checked my cell phone earlier. I also could have found a place to check my email out in this no-cell-no-internet location I am at because that is where the invite was supposed to be sent. I did none of these. I truly regret and am sorry I did not do at least one of them because I truly value my friend but sadly I didn't and I really have no excuse other than to say I made a mistake.

This is reality. There is always, at the very least, one could have done statement. You could have been there. You could have called. You could have told me. You could have found a way. You could have avoided that. Or how about this self-righteous could have that I like to pull out now and again ...You could have given me the same respect I give you. While could have statements always seem to find a place they fall drastically short and meet a dead end in the fact that hindsight is 20/20. In talking about a fellow prisoner in a concentration camp, Victor E. Frankl writes, "No man should judge unless he asks himself in absolute honesty whether in a similar situation he might not have done the same" (68). It is impossible to answer the question Frankl puts forth because we are never able to fully put ourselves in a similar situation, with the same thoughts, same past experiences, same mindset, same beliefs as the one we may be judging.

If I am unable to fully conclude whether I would do the same in a similar situation, there is no way I can judge. If Victor Frankl says this of his experience in a concentration camp there is no reason that I should not be able to adopt the same attitude. The truth is that I can speculate all I want but I can never be sure of my potential judgment. Therefore, there is no way I can hold a friend's remorseful action against them. I hope that my friend allows me this grace in this current missing a birthday mishap, just as my parents allowed me the grace when I slammed our lawn tractor into our truck.

Gracefully Getting an A-

When I received my A- on the research paper, I felt I did not know what I was doing and that I definitely received grace. Looking back, I probably did not deserve the grade I got despite the fact that I still learned a ton from the assignment. My research paper simply did not meet the expectations or exact requirements for the class. However, somehow my very gracious professor saw past the seeming requirements and acknowledged the fact that I was honestly trying my best. The class was, to date, the hardest class I have taken and it did a really good job at attacking my intellectual ego. That class was out of the realm of what I had in my current repertoire of thought and knowledge. Despite the challenge I finished the class, painfully, and only because the professor was gracious enough to put up with a lot of my ignorance.

This is how I want my friendships to be. I want my friends to realize that I really don't have it all together, I will not meet their expectations, and I will hurt them because of this. I do not choose to do this intentionally but because I am ignorant. I do not know it all and will never know it all. I love my friends dearly and I attempt to simply do my best but sometimes I really don't have a clue what I am doing.

One of the greatest examples of this is thinking about Jesus on the cross. Jesus was crucified in the name of saving humanity from our sin. It was humanity's sin that ultimately nailed Him to the cross and, according to the Bible, Jesus did not deserve crucifixion and yet, that's what happened to Him. One of the things that Jesus said when He was crucified was, "Father, forgive them, for they know not what they do" (Luke 23:34). I can hear my own cry in this, "Friends, forgive me, for I know not what I do."

The people who crucified Jesus, caught up in their own ideologies and beliefs, thought they were doing the right thing. Sometimes I also get caught up in my own ideologies and beliefs. Sometimes, I do and say things out of ignorance. Sometimes, I think I am right. Sometimes, I think that I am doing exactly the right thing. Sometimes I think I am responding in the only appropriate way.

But what the hell do I know? What the hell does anyone know about what is going on in another's head and heart? I truly believe and attempt to embrace the thought that people are not out to intentionally cause harm, at least those that I would consider my friends. I believe this is true because as arrogant, cocky, selfish, and prideful as I can be, I know that I don't like to hurt other people, let alone those that I respect on a deeper level. I know that my selfish nature has hurt people. At the same time, I think that if I were to see the outcomes of my actions from the minds and hearts of the one I hurt before I even act, I am convinced, or at least I would hope that, at most times I would act differently. It would save a lot of eating crow.

I am bound to hurt my friends. I know this because I have at one time or another hurt every friend I can think of, at least the ones that matter. I also have been hurt by every friend I can think of, and again, at least the ones that matter. I have decided that if it hurts to love that I am doing it wrong or I am doing it full-heartedly. If it doesn't hurt, it isn't worth it because I know that when it hurts I am standing in the middle of both my friend's and my deepest weakness, brokenness, and rejection, knowing that, "[o]nly when all of our weaknesses are accepted as a part of our humanity can our negative, broken self-images be transformed," (Vanier, *Becoming Human* 26). It is an invitation that speaks, "Forgive them, for they know not what they do."

11

Stealing Fries

I am not one to easily trust people. I am skeptical by nature. I also know that some of my past hurt and brokenness makes me question more about what trust is and how it works. However, I have realized something strange. It is when I can comfortably steal some fries off my friend's plate without asking, and with no negative reaction, that I know that I have reached a certain level of trust. Another level is when a friend can comfortably reach over and take a chip out of the bag of chips that I am holding, without asking and I don't think a negative thing about it. There is some sort of welcoming and inviting assumption made between my friend and I at these moments that tell me there is some level of mutual acceptance and love. I have caught myself taking note of such occasions because for a person who rarely trusts it is a good thing to note. The assumption of sharing food is one measure of trust that I have used. Another is when I notice that manners begin to weaken. It is not that rudeness enters a friendship but I notice that a thank-you or a please become less extravagant. Instead of a, "Thank-you so much for giving me a ride home!!! I really appreciate it!! Walking really does suck!!" it becomes "Thanks man, see ya soon." On top of this are the greater assumptions that begin to be made. The idea that a ride home is just a given, it does not need to be asked or offered. When I notice these tangible things occurring I know that some level of trust has been built between my friend and I.

Trust is priceless. Trust is what intimacy, the ability to be close and deeply connected to another, is built upon. As the level of trust in a relationship increases, more can be invested in the friendship. Sometimes I wish that my naturally skeptical mind, and the hurt and brokenness that serves to inform it, did not hold people as far back as I often do. I have challenged and continue to challenge this assumption. The unfortunate reality is that sometimes my assumption can be proven correct; people can't be trusted. However, this cannot and should not always be the reality and it is within this pain that I have questioned what it means to trust.

It has become quite clear to me that I need to be more secure in my friendships, aka trust my friends more. I went on a road-trip with a great friend a month back and a part of me was nervous. This would be the most consecutive amount of time that I have ever spent with my friend. I worried that at the end of this trip that we would hate each other. In some ways I looked at the trip as a make-it-or-break-it for the relationship that we have built. As we were driving I expressed this fear to my friend and he seemed somewhat surprised. He simply told me that it never crossed his mind. I felt somewhat embarrassed or regretful for even questioning the great friendship we have.

I am also partially responsible for wrecking a great friendship because of a lack of trust. It can be quite easy to avoid trust completely. There are two things a person needs to do in order to avoid trust. One, you need to create the most confident, secure, and collected persona that you can. You will appear wonderful and great, and people will say, just as one friend said to me, "I never bothered trying to be your friend because you seemed like you had enough." Second, you need to be willing to face a constant barrage of loneliness. I have done these two things, heck, maybe I still do. It's not what it's cracked up to be.

I need to trust my friends and my friends need to have the ability to trust me. As lame as it is, I am going to refer to the definition of trust that my Microsoft Word 2004 offers me: "[C]onfidence in and reliance on good qualities, especially fairness, truth, honor, or ability." That means that I if I am to trust, all I need to do is to have confidence in and reliance on my friends' ability to be fair, truthful, and honorable, and vice versa.

Okay. That is easy enough. To be honest, all that comes to mind is the logic and possibly the old saying, "You want something done, do it yourself." So, following that logic, I will rely on my own ability to be fair, truthful, and honorable in order to have a good and deep friendship with someone else. I will not only be fair, truthful, and honorable for my friend's sake, I will also be fair, truthful and honorable for my own sake. How kind of me. My friends can simply be tokens of my strong ego.

If this is the logic I follow, eventually I will end up as the crotchety and bitter old miser that only knows how to tell the neighbor kids to get off his lawn and criticizes everyone with his superior intellect because he knows what life is all about. Lack of trust can be a breeding ground for arrogance and pride. If people cannot be trusted, at some level I know that, at least for myself, I am making a statement that everyone else must be sub par. How dare I insult my friends like that?

However, there is another person I could become. I could also become a kind but overbearing and alone old bachelor that sings to himself the Everly Brothers song, "When will I be loved?" every night before he goes to bed, all the while wondering what is wrong with him. Lack of trust can also be a breeding ground for loneliness. In the search to be loved, I would wonder what it is about me that makes me unlovable and, all the while and somewhat ironically, it was not that I was unlovable but that I turned away the very love I searched for by not being willing to trust.

On the other end of the spectrum, if I don't allow myself to be trustworthy, I could become an old, lonely, narcissistic bachelor that expects everyone to cater to me. If I am not willing to let people trust me, and am completely unreliable but am willing to trust others, it would be quite easy to become quite selfish. Lack of trust could become a breeding ground for selfishness.

These three possible outcomes, amongst probably many more undesirable ones, should not be risked. This means I need to face those things that get in the way of trust. In regards to allowing myself to trust, I have narrowed it down to three different factors: Hurt, pride, and fear. In regards to allowing myself to be trustworthy, I have decided that when it comes down to it, it can be summarized with a statement from the Bible, "Whoever can be trusted with very little can also be trusted with much, and whoever is dishonest with very little will also be dishonest with much"(Luke 16:10). Let me divulge on all of his.

Hurt

I was a chubby, shy teen and during this time I had to change schools. It is not easy for a chubby, shy teen to make new friends, let alone avoid being teased and harassed. I was the one that you would see playing Simcity at lunchtime, alone. Looking back, there is probably not much lower I could have been placed on the social ladder. However, eventually I did make it up a rung or two but at a great cost. I needed friends so badly at that time that I learned that I needed to do everything and anything for my friends and never expect anything back. With my shyness working against me, my friends, or the group that I hung out with, never made an attempt or had a chance to truly know me. Besides their making fun of me occasionally, they simply tolerated having me around. My acceptance became more important than my self-worth. Harassment became something I had to tolerate. At times I was quite literally uninvited to certain events and at school dances the girls in my friend group would make excuses as to why they could not dance with me, only to find them minutes later dancing with someone else. During the days at school, I would collect all the strength I had, being as confident and as together as I could. It was water off a duck's back. During the evenings I remember crumbling in tears, convincing myself that it was a normal and healthy thing to cry everyday.

I do not paint this picture of pain to create sympathy but to illustrate how much hurt can impact trust. In experiencing this pain, I learned a couple of unhealthy things about trust. I learned that in order to have a friend I needed to be as honorable and as good a friend as I could without ever expecting anything back. My friends could trust me but I did not necessarily need to trust them. To be trusted became synonymous with friendship but to be able to trust was a luxury. Second, I learned to trust that if I did my best to be the best friend I could be then I could simply be tolerated. It really did not seem worth the extra effort to trust people based on the fact that it hurt enough already to trust them while simply being tolerated. If I trusted them with more, how much more pain would I be causing myself?

I have worked through most of this pain but as I reflect now, I am struck by remnants. This pain happened at a crucial time in my development, when acceptance with peers is high. There always may be remnants of this pain, the way I view and process trust, but this is where awareness is key. For those friendships and relationships that are important, the ones that are growing, I need to be aware that sometimes this past pain, the way my mind has and can twist trust, may be creating disorder. I cannot simply let the pain from my past dictate how my current relationships will go.

Pride

I am not going to lie. I know that I learned a lot about being the best friend a person can be from the pain

I experienced during my teenage years. I made a vow during that time that I would be everything that those that I was harassed by weren't. I learned how to be a good friend. I learned how to be a **very** good friend. It is strange to say but at times I have had to challenge myself to not be as good a friend. Not because it's not a good thing to be a good friend but because it has been an unhealthy habit for me to allow myself to simply be the doormat.

There was a time when I prided myself on how good a friend I could be. I found a great deal of self-worth in the friend I could be. This was shattered one day however, when I realized that part of being a good friend was not only being trustworthy but also trusting. If I did not trust my friends, I was really not a good friend at all. This was a horribly great realization.

Pride steps in the way of trust because if I know best, if I know how to do relationship best, if I am the most trustworthy person there is, there is very little room for anyone else to be trusted. It goes back to the idea that I mentioned earlier, that if you want something done, you do it yourself. And as I reflected on before, this is not possible in a friendship. I need to constantly remind myself of the obvious, I do not know better than anyone else.

Fear

It is obvious and far from profound to say that there is fear in trusting. Trusting involves opening up and letting another hold a piece of my fragility. If I trust another with a piece of my fragility, there is a risk that they might hurt it or cause harm. There is nothing more to say about this fear than to say that I need to challenge myself to step through this.

There is another great fear in trusting, the fear of change. I think that in a lot of relationships a certain equilibrium is reached so that it becomes hard to step further into trust and depth. I know that for myself it is easier to remain on the common ground that a friendship is based or built upon than to challenge myself and trust my friendly counterpart with the things that are different. To trust my friend with elements of myself that are foreign to the friendship, or to the commonality that we share, interrupts the equilibrium of the friendship. If my friend shares something out of the ordinary, it may require more of me, or if I share more it may require more of my friend and this will upset the equilibrium that our friendship is.

I once reached a point in a friendship that became greatly troublesome. There are elements of my friend and myself that were exposed. The equilibrium that our friendship had become was disrupted. Sadly, instead of confronting this change something strange happened. A distance was created and it was as if we were both pretending we weren't as close of friends as we were. There was an elephant in room, in our friendship, but neither of us acknowledged it and we simply backed away because to acknowledge it meant change, a change that neither of us were willing to embrace. Jean Vanier writes that, "To be human is to create sufficient order so that we can move on into insecurity and seeming disorder. In this way, we discover the new" (*Becoming Human* 13). Trust demands change because it is ever growing. A friendship that does not challenge the equilibrium verges on the mundane and becomes stagnant.

To Be Trusted

So, in regards to being trusted, I mentioned earlier the verse from the bible that says, "Whoever can be trusted with very little can also be trusted with much, and whoever is dishonest with very little will also be dishonest with much."(Luke 16:10). To get this train of thought to completion, I need to combine the thought in this verse with the definition of trust that I used earlier: "[C]onfidence in and reliance on good qualities, especially fairness, truth, honor, or ability."

The combination of these two thoughts dictates that in order to build trust and to be trustworthy I need to first be fair, truthful, and honorable with the small things that my friends entrust me with. I need to communicate to my friends that I am going to be fair, truthful, and honorable, and in the general sense a good person. As they see I am good to them in the smallest areas, they can begin to offer me greater pieces of themselves. It then becomes a cycle whereby I prove my goodness to them and they then entrust me with more.

It's odd as I reflect on what it requires in order to be trusted, as it seems far from profound. Of course no one would trust me if I wasn't at least decently good to them. I would have a hard time trusting anyone that was a complete asshole to me. However, I suppose there should be nothing profound about the fact that we should be good to each other.

I have decided that it simply comes down to knowing another's heart, and seeing a genuine care and concern that communicates no harm or hurt is intended. The love

we put forth and offer to another is simply an invitation
to be trusted and an inquiry of whether we can trust.

12

Awkward Cousin Phase

Growing up, my family and I occasionally visited some extended family that lived about six hour away. We probably only visited once or twice a year. Over the years, I began to notice a very strange occurrence surrounding these visits. I have labeled this reoccurring event as awkward cousin phase. It always occurred during the first ten to fifteen minutes of arriving. While the details always varied slightly, this is how it would often go. We would all say our hellos and the adults would begin to visit. My siblings and our cousins would all remain somewhat quiet until one of the adults would tell us to go play. We would then go to another room, the living room maybe, where we would again remain quiet, staring at each other. This would go on for about two minutes until one of us was brave enough to make the first move to a toy, thereby initiating arguably the closest intimacy two children can enjoy, happily playing together. It was like magic because once that first move was made everyone followed suit and we became like best friends within minutes. When it came time to make the six hour drive back a day or two later, we would be almost in tears leaving.

I have thought about this occurrence a fair bit and I have realized that I do this on a regular basis with my friends, even my closest ones. In an awkward cousin phase I get together with friends and there is an initial time of reacquainting that happens. We talk about stuff, any stuff, but nothing of real relevance, almost as if we were staring at each other quietly, figuring each other out, just as I remember as a kid. Then something magical happens, someone makes the first move to the real stuff by putting out a statement that requires vulnerability and trust, like making the first move to the toy and initiating the first act of play. And then we are the best of friends again and when the time comes to part ways an appreciation and gratitude pours forth combined with sadness that we have to part ways so soon.

Awkward cousin phase has its place because it allows for a time of reacquainting and of feeling out the headspace of another. It is a time of dropping guards and opening up, letting loose like undoing your belt after a big Christmas dinner. It is a valuable part but it is also important to me and I think for the sake of any good friendship that I get past awkward cousin phase, at least once and awhile. Sometimes it can be too easy just to remain in awkward cousin phase talking about the weather when deep down both my friend and I need our hearts spoken to. Getting past awkward cousin phase speaks to me about overcoming those things that block me from the real stuff, intimacy, the giving and receiving of love.

The Giving of Love

In a basic sense, I will argue, we all have the ability to know right from wrong, good from evil. I know that even in the most selfish of my actions, I could tell you whether or not my action was good or caring to another. Take, for example, my cousin who recently was offered a job providing loans to low-income families at an interest rate of 30%. He could have taken this job quite easily because the salary was quite nice, however, morally he could not wrap his head around the idea of providing a loan to these low-income families that would take an eternity to pay off, with the great potential of only worsening their overall situations. If anyone took even two minutes to honestly put themselves in the shoes of those low-income families, I feel it would become quite obvious that a 30% interest rate on a loan is far from fair. This is how I see my ability to love. If I were to put myself in the shoes of those that receive whatever I throw at them, words, actions, or whatever, I will be able to know if it was kind, caring, or loving of me or not. The Bible describes love as being patient and kind; saying it does not envy, does not boast, and is not proud, rude, self-seeking, easily angered; and it keeps no record of wrongs (1 Corinthians 13:4-5). All of these make sense to me if I take a few minutes to think about them. I can't say I am good at any of them at times, or that I couldn't polish up my ability and skill in loving but there is something internal within me that knows how to be a good person to someone, communicating care and concern. As well, often I will be able to tell by the reaction from my friendly counterpart whether my action or word was loving or not.

At the same time, I do not want to minimize the act of loving because there is so much more to it than I am saying quite simply. I say this because after writing that last paragraph and putting myself in the shoes of a reader, it could seem quite insulting to some, maybe even to myself. The act of loving speaks of so much more! It speaks of commitment and, at many times, sacrifice, often amidst the pain and hurt that relationship can entail when two people perfectly flawed come together.

To love is vulnerable. To love is to invite another close in order that we might give to them. To have someone close can be a fearful event because we chance being rejected, often for another. It is a greater version of that feeling you get when you see someone waving at you so you wave back only to find out that they were waving at someone behind you. You were well intentioned and friendly in your wave but it was not received, and you are left looking like an idiot. Love is when one places the care, concern, and appreciation of another above their own fear of rejection and pain. Sometimes this means looking like a complete fool or idiot, stepping into and walking through the most painful places of vulnerability or darkness.

This reflection explains to me why I have heard the saying, "Love is a choice, not a feeling." If loving risks the pain of being vulnerable or looking like an idiot, and knowing that I never feel like being in pain or looking like an idiot, it must be within my mental capacities that I choose to step into this risk. I may know the practicalities of loving someone, like calling a friend on their birthday or truly and genuinely inquiring about certain aspects of their life, but actually doing these acts may require an intentional and conscious decision that may involve being rejected or turned away. Or simply stated, to love is easier said than done.

Let me give an example that both illustrates and deepens this thought. I have a friend that called me in tears in the middle of the night. To say the least, he needed someone to talk to. It is easy to say that to love my friend in this situation, all I would have to do is offer a listening ear, express my concern, offer some encouragement, and see where the conversation goes. That is the practical part of loving friend. Doing this was not as easy. I noticed that as the conversation went on, I started to feel quite exposed and vulnerable myself. He was the one in tears but in order to communicate my concern and appreciation for him I needed to say things that could be met with rejection. On the surface level, one would think that expressing appreciation and words of encouragement should not be met with rejection but below the surface I began to fear that maybe they would not be good enough. Maybe, if I open up and express love and appreciation to my friend, it won't be good enough for him. If it is not good enough, maybe I am not good enough, not good enough to be his friend. I think sometimes I not only avoid expressing my love towards someone based on a fear of rejection but also on a fear of not being good enough.

Who am I to think that I could ever completely fulfill the needs of a broken human heart in my own human brokenness? I read that "the only way to have unconditional love is to recognize and admit that you sometimes have conditions blocking your love" (Bloomfield 57). I need to be able to admit, and be honest with myself in that I will never and can't be the perfect friend. So, if someone is unwilling to accept this fact, or unwilling to accept parts of my broken attempt to love, I will face the risk I took in loving, that I may be rejected. I will settle on being the idiot who attempted to wave at someone who I thought was waving at me.

Taking Love

I think within my top ten, maybe top twenty, movies is the 80s movie *The Breakfast Club*. The basic plot line is five teenagers, of varying stereotypes, who meet in detention. I find it fascinating because as their time in detention progresses, the stereotypes keeping them apart begin to crumble. One of my favorite quotable interactions is when Allison asks Claire, "Why are you being so nice to me?"

"Because you're letting me," responds Claire.

This quote reminds me that there is love out there, freely offered, but sometimes I shut myself off from it and then, somehow, I can catch myself beginning to wonder whether there is anyone that really loves me. There are many things that I have come to be quite aware of that I do in order to distance myself from people's love. We all protect our hearts, and rightfully so as we do live in a broken world. We also protect based on the perceived level, or foundation, of trust that we have built with a person. There is probably no way I would tell my deepest and darkest secrets, whatever they may be, to a stranger on the street despite how nice, genuine, authentic, and loving they may seem to be. Beyond these necessary protective moments are the moments when I refuse to accept the gift of love and care from those that actually do care. These are the moments I would like to explore.

Back in high school, I had the hugest crush on a girl named Kelly, which just happens to rhyme with Shelley if you were wondering. During this time in my life I listened to a song by Barney Bentall a lot called "Oh Shelly," which naturally I changed to "Oh Kelly." In listening to and singing my version of the song "Oh Kelly," I was always struck by the lyrics, "It's not how much you love, please remember that's not how a heart is judged, it's about letting someone love you in return." This is a love song in which Barney Bentall sings about being torn up because the one he loved wouldn't let him love. I have been in this place and I have said to myself, "How dare you decide how much I love and care?"

I have a great friend. He is generous, giving, loving, and often has spoken immense truth into my life. He is admirable and has given me nothing but respect and yet, at times I have wondered why it is that I do not value his friendship as much as I do the friendships I have with others. It is not that I do not appreciate what he has done for me but I am becoming conscious of the fact that he never drops his guard. He remains a strong wall, seemingly confident and secure, and I never have the opportunity to love him back. I want to have the ability to love and care back but he never appears that he needs me.

I do this. I create a front, portraying myself as calm, collected, confident, together. Just like my friend, this front tells the people around me that they need not worry about me, they need not care for me, they need not worry about giving back to me. Why would I do this? There are only two options that I feel are possible. I am either above or below the love that those around me might offer. To be above it would speak of a pride and arrogance, or a social status, which is unreachable even to the most perfect and complete person out there. I cannot in any right mind say that I am complete and perfect enough that I do not need the love of my fellow humans. To be below the love speaks of being unworthy of it. How could I be unworthy of something like mutual human love if I myself am a human? It is also quite irrational. If I cannot make the excuse that "Oh, I am good, don't worry about me, I have what I need, I don't need love," then it must be that there is a part of me that feels unworthy of the love that people offer.

If someone were to ask me if I was unworthy of love or unlovable, I would immediately answer with a resounding and defensive, "No!" However, as I think about it now, I don't know how else to rationally explain some of my actions or some of the experiences from my past. How else do I explain my unwillingness at times to allow myself to receive the love that people offer? Or how do I process what I learned when I was a chubby teenager, who had to move to a new school, that in order to have friends, amidst being torn down verbally, I had to give and give and never expect to get anything back. I had to give and give and then be eternally grateful that my friends even tolerated having me around. This experience alone tells me that I learned that I was unworthy of the love of those around me. It is impossible to not think that something that happened during a crucial year in my development would still have an affect on me today in some way.

This being said, I have no choice but to admit that there is a part of me rejecting the love that people offer out of the belief that I am unworthy or not worth their effort. It's as if in accepting the love that people offer, I am being a burden or a hassle. The most obvious place I notice my rejection of love is when I apologize rather than say thank you. Instead of saying thank you when my friend offers a listening ear, I say, "Sorry for throwing all of this on you." Instead of saying thank you when a friend goes out of his or her way for me, I say, "Oh, sorry that you had to do that for me, going out of your way and all." Or I will say, "You shouldn't have done that." Instead of appreciating the gift offered, I turn myself into a burden.

I get my nose a little out of joint when people do this to me. If I want to give you something, offer you something, love you, accept it graciously! First of all, I would not offer something if I truly did not want you to receive it! Second, when I hear a statement like, "Sorry for throwing all of this on you" after I have listened intently to you for an hour, I get somewhat perturbed. I get a little perturbed because all of a sudden the fact that I listened to you, the gift that I offered, is taken from me and turned into something I had to do, or was obliged to do, or was forced to do. How dare you limit my gift in that way?

I have a gift in being hypocritical so I have begun to challenge myself to say thank you instead of I'm sorry. I look at it as making myself a burden because I am worth it. If I am not too good for the love of another, and I am not below it and unworthy of it, it is only appropriate that I let others around love me. Letting myself be loved goes hand in hand with loving others. It is not an and/or situation.

In allowing myself to become a burden to others, I am realizing that just as loving requires vulnerability so does being loved. I was sharing deeply with a good friend one day and he said to me, "Wow, this is the first time I have ever seen you be vulnerable. You always seem to have life together." I found this statement troubling because a part of me believed that just because I was sharing information about myself, I was being vulnerable, even if it was things I had never told anyone before. I was partially mistaken because the very act of being vulnerable requires exposure to possible pain, emotional or physical. If I simply offer elements of my life that I have figured out, that I have a grasp on, whether I tell only few people or not, is not being vulnerable. If they don't have the ability to hurt me, based on the information I tell, I am not being vulnerable. Take, for example, if someone tells me that they are really self-conscious about their weight. This is vulnerability because I could call him Fatty-McFatty Pants and quite possibly hurt him. However, if the person told me that when he was young that he was very self-conscious about his or her weight, it is not as vulnerable, possibly at all. I could call him Fatty-McFatty Pants and he may not even care in the slightest.

In order to be loved, I need to allow myself to be vulnerable. Ultimately I need to be loved the most in the areas that I perceive to be unlovable and these also happen to be the areas of vulnerability. Unless I am willing to open up, my friends don't have the ability to really love me. If I choose to only expose those parts of myself that are collected, together, and strong, I can easily create a sense of false intimacy with my friends. I will rely on the fact that they are willing to spend time with me and are willing to listen to my stories but under the surface I will never know if they truly love me until they see those parts of me that are most vulnerable.

I could explore this avenue of giving and receiving love for an eternity. There are so many facets of love and intimacy that are of intrigue and interest. I could delve deeply into every crack and crevice but the reality is that sometimes the only and best thing to do is to simply live, challenging myself to love and be loved, entering into relationships with the intent of knowing and being known. It always starts shallow and always has the possibility of going deep. I realize that sometimes I forget about this and expect depth that is not there yet, becoming dissatisfied and wondering where the depth is. I can talk about the weather, I can talk about work, I can talk about my plans for the weekend but sometimes I want more. I am realizing however that these everyday details can and are more. The everyday details can be a sacred launch pad to depth if I allow them to be, just like awkward cousin phase is a starting point to get to the real stuff in life.

13

Rules of Engagement and Stumbling Drunks

There are quite a few topics in this book that I have had difficulty writing about because of the vulnerability and exposure of myself to myself. While somewhat therapeutic is was also uncomfortable. I don't like to acknowledge that I don't have life all together nor have I met anyone that does like to admit this. It gets heavy at times. This specific chapter is no different except this chapter also begins to and makes my blood curdle. This is the chapter when I talk about how despite even the mere shot in the dark chance that perfection in all that I have talked about thus far, as well as the things I didn't talk about, were reached, sometimes broken relationships still happen. It makes my blood curdle because despite what I do or attempt to do, I am at the will of other people's best efforts, knowing full well that not even I can, nor am I willing, to do my best at times. I will argue that a broken relationship is the saddest human tragedy that I know because, while hurt and pain are unavoidable in a relationship, meeting in the middle should always be an option. There is no logical and rational reason or excuse that two people, apart from mentally unhealthy and abusive situations, should part ways with a lack of respect and dignity for the other and yet, I see it happen all of the time.

More recently I have been attempting to the best of my ability to keep my heart from growing callous towards anyone. This means everything from whitewashing people with labels like selfish, arrogant, or ignorant, to not letting the hurts I have experienced be used as excuses to push people away. When I let my heart grow callous, I find that I risk too much. I risk becoming prideful and arrogant because the only conclusion I can make in writing someone off and allowing myself to grow callous towards someone is that I know better, I was right, and that he or she really just doesn't know how to do life. Subsequently, the one I have allowed myself to grow callous towards becomes a two-dimensional character, whereby all I can see is what I have written him or her off for. This someone becomes whitewashed with a label like arrogant, selfish, or ignorant. And I suppose that this person very well could be these labels as we all are but I never want that to be the only thing that I see in another fellow human being. Inappropriate and misplaced labels are not only what is at the heart of disrespect but is what invites it. We are all worth more respect and dignity than this.

Rules of Engagement

I always wonder how the greatest of relationships can end up in a train wreck. The way that I have come to process this revolves around what I have come to label as rules of engagement. From the moment we make first contact with someone, we begin an unspoken negotiation process. We negotiate everything from how often to call, where and when we are welcome, where we hang out, from what we do together to how close the relationship is and how close we allow ourselves to become. In a basic sense, it is getting to know someone, except it goes a bit deeper than that. It becomes the expectations, whether we are consciously aware of them or not, that define the relationship. They are also the elements that we begin to trust and rely on in the friendship. For example, I will begin to trust and get used to the fact that when I text you that you always text me back. Or, you will begin to trust that I may not talk to you for a few days, not replying to your texts, but then eventually will get back to you and we will get together, catching up on everything that may have been missed.

These are what I call the rules of engagement. We all have unspoken rules that get written as we enter a relationship with anyone. They become basic assumptions and expectations that become lubricant for the relationship. There are two things that I believe happen to make great relationships turn into train wrecks. First, one of the two parties in a relationship change the rules of engagement without negotiating it. Second, one of the two parties places a rule of engagement on a relationship that was not negotiated. Relationships can come to a crashing halt, or maybe a passive-aggressive and apathetic discontinuity, when one of these two options happen. When you don't know what to expect, or what is expected of you, or how your relationship is supposed to work, all chaos can break loose. Confusion and hurt lead to questions of doubt and trust.

I had a friend who for a time I would have called my best friend. We spent a significant amount of time together. I got used to this and I got used to at least hearing from him everyday, even if it was as simple as a late night text wishing me a good night. In the times we never made contact, sometimes for days, there was always the assumption that it did not matter and that we would talk when we talked. There was a great sense of freedom built around a great level of trust. I never questioned the friendship because what we had negotiated was one that allowed for a very close relationship but was not clingy, fused, or overbearing. I felt so free to simply be who I was, with great room to be my independent self.

And then something changed, within a month. It was as if I fell off the face of the planet. My friend would hardly talk to me anymore. It was like pulling teeth to get him to hang out. We could not see each other for a few days and when we would meet again, it was as if we were strangers. About this same time, he began to spend more and more time with some other people. I did not understand. This was not what our friendship was. I inquired as to what was going on and he apologized, telling me that he didn't realize that he was doing this. This gap, and distance, that was created remained. I was hurt but more so I just missed my friend.

On top of this, I had no idea what to do because life circumstances required us to be in the same place at the

same time several times a week. The rules of
engagement had changed. He changed them without
telling me. I did not get the memo. According to how our
friendship worked, this current predicament was nothing I
expected. I no longer knew how I was supposed to act.
Was I also supposed to pretend that he no longer existed?
This may have been the smart option but I do not give up
on good friendship that easy, or some may argue at all.
Amidst this, I was told to not worry or question our
friendship. I did not understand. If he actually took the
time and explained to me what was going on, why he
would not talk to me anymore, why he wouldn't hang out,
why I began to be excluded from things that I normally
wouldn't have, then maybe a new set of rules of
engagement could have been negotiated. Maybe there
was a reason behind his strange actions that I was
unaware of, something that would explain the change in
the rules of engagement. Instead a ludicrous game of cat
and mouse ensued, whereby I was left in the dark about
the demise of our friendship.

Another piece of this could be that I put a rule of
engagement on the great friendship we had that was not
negotiated. It could very well be that a part of this train
wreck resulted from me expecting something that I
thought was a given in our friendship. It could be that I
threw on a rule of engagement that asked for more than
what was there. In a basic sense, expecting something
that was never present in our friendship before but that I
assumed would be.

The reality is that it is impossible to avoid these rules
of engagement because they are what make our
relationships go smoothly. Avoidance will unavoidably
lead to confusion at some point because human behavior,

and imperfection, dictates that rules are made to be broken. On top of which we all bring with us a bag full of rules of engagement that unavoidably will be pulled out at some point in every relationship.

Relationships crumble and become the train wrecks they are because we become unwilling to meet and understand each other. And this is the blood curdling sad part; there is no reason for this. I hatefully frown in disgust at the times that I have written people off in my arrogant ignorance, and I painfully scream out in tears and for vengeance when I have been written off. There has got to be more than this because I don't want to live with the heaviness that arrogant ignorance can be. I also don't want to carry the weight of the bitterness that tears and vengeance encompass.

The Heaviness of Arrogant Ignorance

I don't want to carry arrogance because it places superiority between my neighbor and I. I don't want to distance people in superiority because the more I do so the easier it will become to do so in the future. On top of which arrogant ignorance is not very flattering, or so my friends tell me, ha. This means there has to be an alternative.

I am calling this alternative humility. K'naan, a rapper from Somalia, in his song *Take a Minute* raps, "And any man who knows a thing knows he knows not a damn, damn thing at all." I like this line a lot because if I internalize it, it allows me, in my arrogant ignorance, first to acknowledge that I actually know something, stroking my ego, and then it strips away my need to hold on to whatever I am arrogantly ignorant about by telling me I know nothing. There is great wisdom in this line, the same wisdom I need to bring to my relationships. When I find myself thinking that I know exactly what is going on in a hurting friendship, or when I make conclusions in surety, I need to realize that while I may have ability to process and analyze information, I do no know everything. In fact, I probably know not a damn, damn thing at all.

Added to the wonderful lyrics by K'naan is the idea captured in what Jean Vanier writes,

> Weakness, recognized, accepted, and offered, is at the heart of belonging, so it is at the heart of communion with another. Weakness carries within it a secret power. The cry and the trust that flow from weakness can open up hearts. The one who is weaker can call forth powers of love in the one who is stronger. (*Becoming Human* 40)

If I am willing to step forward and admit the weakest parts of myself, my vulnerability, I can avoid fueling the fire that causes train wreck relationships with my arrogant ignorance. If I simply come as a broken human being, I would hope that that is also what I will find in the other. In a troubled relationship, we too quickly offer what we know is wrong with the other person and what they need to do, instead of first offering where we are broken and hurt. At times all we want is for the relationship to be restored but all we do is tear it down, remaining arrogantly ignorant.

The Weight of Bitterness and Vengeance

There is little we can do when we are written off. It can be like talking to a wall. I have done this and do this.

I have thought about it and, in all honesty, being unwilling to reconcile or make peace can be a form of abuse because it forces the one wanting to reconcile or make peace into a place where he or she almost has no choice but to harden his or her heart and grow callous towards the other. I don't want to be callous towards anyone because it is the breeding ground of bitterness and invites arrogant disrespect.

However, sometimes there is no choice, we may find ourselves written off. In order to stay free of being callous and to release myself from being backed too much into a heart-hardening corner, the only option I see is grace. I need to be willing to simply say and admit the truth that neither my former friendly counterpart nor I have all the facts right. This concept is similar to the humility that I discussed above in regards to the K'naan lyrics. However, it goes further because this humility chooses to believe that hidden behind all the horrible things about the broken relationship train wreck is that there is still the same person that was once your dear friend. Your friend still has the same gifts, talents, and great things about him or her as they did before. It is choosing to not be blinded by the many small or big things you were hurt by.

I had a professor that used the quote, "Forgiveness is free and reconciliation is earned." I think this is true and I would like to live it. I will offer forgiveness, and forgive, never expecting reconciliation but always inviting it. This is hard to do because it asks that I keep a small part of my heart open to the one that hurt me and risk once again being hurt.

I have asked myself why I might do this and the only answer that I can come up with is this, and I said it earlier. One of the things that Jesus said as, or when, He was crucified was, "Father, forgive them, for they know not what they do"(Luke 23:34). I can hear my own cry in this, "Friends, forgive me, for I know not what I do." I know that at times I don't know what I am doing and I hurt the people I love. I also know that I have written people off, ruining friendships, because I thought I knew what I was doing. I want and need grace so badly. I need it so badly that I can't do anything but offer it back.

Final Thoughts

Broken relationships are painful. Relationships in general can be painful. All I know is that I get so frustrated because when it comes down to it, we are all a bunch of stumbling drunks when it comes to relationship. We do the best we can to keep our balance and our footing as we walk together. Inevitable we fall, we stagger into each other, and we stumble apart only to drift back together a time later. It's annoying because, just like drunks, we can get agitated too easily and quickly before we have the opportunity to truly understand what is going on, completely missing the heart of the other person walking with you. Sometimes we need to be willing to try to sober up with a cup of coffee while we once again find our bearings as friends.

14

The Importance of Sitting at Home Alone and Lonely in a 70s Armchair

It was what only can be called a horrible family heirloom, the brown 70s rocking armchair that was passed from my grandparents to my Aunt and Uncle, onto my cousin and his wife, back to the possession of my Aunt and Uncle, then passed on to me where it eventually and unfortunately met its demise. I am unsure whether to call it a family heirloom or a burden as it did serve its sitting purpose for over 30 years. I sat many hours in this chair over my lifetime, until one day it met its lack of need with a hammer and a utility knife. This was a delightful process. I loved that chair. I loved how if you didn't line the swivel legs up properly it would tip over backwards, and how the brown upholstery was faded and worn in places to an almost crisp golden color. It had character. However, with every swing of the hammer and every cut of the utility knife, there was a releasing of bits and parts of my past, expressing frustration, pain, and hurt. That chair played an important part in my journey but being able to fit it into five garbage bags was a surmounting victory. It was a victory because it symbolized a priceless truth of profoundly stepping beyond my own identity and embracing a reality that I never knew. It is obvious that an armchair alone could not have this impact but let me tell you about the importance of sitting at home alone and lonely in a 70s armchair.

I have mentioned before my misfortune resulting from being a chubby, shy teenager in an exterior focused society. This is, in many ways, where this story needs to begin. During that time I hated being teased and bugged, knowing full well I had more to offer to others than my chubby exterior seemed to portray, my shyness being my only defense. It was about this time that I came across a song by the Smashing Pumpkins called "1979." I listened to this song again and again and again for the one lyric that said, "[C]ool kids never have the time." I despised the cool kids. I liked this line a lot because it spoke to me about the arrogance of those that unjustly looked down on me. It told me that within arrogance and pride there was no time for those around you. Arrogance and pride are self-indulgent and this is all I began to see in those that held their noses in the air, refusing to get to know me. It was from this moment that I claimed I would become the cool kid that did have time. I would attempt to be the best friend I could be to everyone and anyone, well almost everyone and anyone. Out of the pain of rejection, I would never make time for the cool kids that never had time for me. I would reject those who rejected, quite the impossible undertaking.

Fast forward to my life as an adult. That vow I made came unmistakably with me into my adult life. I never knew how much until that moment of sitting on that 70s armchair but before I get to that I need to tell you more about how seamless that vow fit into my life and became my identity. I prided myself on being the best friend I could be. At times, I did everything I could to win the favour of people, even if I had to be a doormat. I fed off of statements I heard like, "You are such a good guy," or "I don't know a person who doesn't like you," making them a part of my identity. As far as I was concerned, I was the cool kid who had the time. I would write people off within a couple of minutes if I detected a sniff of arrogance or pride because they weren't worth my time.

This all began to come into question one week when a string of random events occurred that can only be explained as something fate would have. I was stood up on a date because she said I was aloof. I had a cutting dialogue with a very good friend that left me realizing that I was not as good of a friend as I thought. I partook in an exercise during a class that I was taking that made me reflect on my worth and value, and then circumstantially ended up watching a video during the same week that challenged the way people identify themselves and where they place their identity. All of this was on top of an already life questioning doubt and frustration. I felt literally crushed after this week.

I felt like my identity and who I defined myself to be, the good friend, the good guy, the cool kid that did have the time, was falling apart. I began to realize that in all my efforts to be the best friend to anyone and everyone, I spread myself thin, neglecting my own needs in order to be a good friend. I lost myself wondering, "When will I be loved?" I felt as though I was everyone's friend but no one was my friend. I felt an exhaustion that left me crumbled and void of life. Restlessness and tears became my only outlet.

And then, the moment we have been all been waiting for happened. I was sitting at home alone and lonely in that beloved 70s armchair. I sat down on that armchair, attempting to escape the restlessness that I was feeling. Within the silence of the room and the quietness within my soul, tears began to flow. I didn't stop for a long time, and then I began to ask and cry out that there has to be more than this and I can't remain like this. I prayed to God for freedom from the wretchedness that I was feeling.

I began to think about the current moment I was in and began to ask myself what was so deeply wrong with the present. I was sitting comfortably in the family heirloom with no one around to demand anything of me, no one to reject me, no one to be arrogant and prideful. In the comfort of that armchair, I sighed a breath of relief as I began to ask how I defined my worth and identity. If it was not in being the best friend to everyone and anyone, what was it? For years I relied on being the cool kid that had the time, finding my self-worth and my identity in being the best friend I could be. It turns out it was something that I perceived to be an ability. I do have the ability to be a good friend but not to everyone. Besides, part of being a good friend involves letting myself be loved, which I rarely allowed, or had the time for.

My worth had to extend beyond any friendship or relationship. And as I sat there I thought about how it had to extend beyond a gift or a talent, or beyond anything I might currently be good at. It had to extend beyond what I do or what I say, or who I think I am. All of these things are not permanent and if they are not permanent they cannot be relied upon for my worth. If I placed my worth in the ability to make great speeches and for some mistaken reason lost my voice, then all of a sudden I would seemingly have no worth. Or, if I placed my worth in something like how good I could be at tying balloon animals and lost my hand, again I would seemingly have no worth. Or, what if I placed my worth in my ability to think and then lost my mind in some case of permanent amnesia, again... seemingly no worth.

Then, I began to think about what people place their worth in. Things like job, position, acceptance, belonging, knowledge, task, ability, status, appearance, popularity, authority, and possessions came to mind. As I went through the list, none of them seemed like a reliable source of self-worth to form an identity around. And so, I sat there on the brown 70s armchair emptying myself of worthless ideals. It came down to the thought that there has to be something inherent within who I am that does not ever and cannot ever be affected by the world around me, something that can never be stolen or taken.

I turned to a book that has proven quite wise and found two things that struck me as profound. The first is this,

> You see, at just the right time, when we were still powerless, Christ died for the ungodly. Very rarely will anyone die for a righteous man, though

> for a good man someone might possibly dare to
> die. But God demonstrates his own love for us in
> this: While we were still sinners, Christ died for
> us. (Romans 5:5-8)

This thought is something that extended beyond me and beyond the world around me. It tells me that when I was both powerless and still a sinner, basically saying that when my human weakness, imperfection, and brokenness are still clearly present, someone chose to die for me. The second thought that struck me was this, "You were bought at a price; do not become slaves of men" (1 Corinthians 7:23). This second thought informs the first and communicates that because of Christ's death, there is no way I should be a slave to man and that was exactly what I was doing. And if I were to put my worth in and place my identity on any human standard or measure, I run the risk of becoming a slave of man. If I was to place my worth on how well I did my job, for example, creating my identity around it, I am slave to my work because it binds me as I am nothing without it. I have to perform, I have to do well, I have to prove myself otherwise I am nothing. I am a slave.

Where is my worth then? God was the only answer I could come up with. I hate sounding cliché but in that moment as I sat nestled in that brown 70s armchair, a peace began to settle upon me that I can only describe as Holy. Everything around me began to fade and all that remained was me, whoever it was, and an existence beyond me that communicated to me worth. I could have sat in that chair, having never talked to anyone in my whole life, having never done anything in my whole life, having no influence or connection with anyone and yet I was important. My existence became a statement of the

marvel and wonder of the human species as flawed, or as
broken, or as weak as I am. I had inherent worth not
because of anything I was, am, or ever could be, but
because of an existence beyond me that chose to create
me, evolve me, and love me to the point of death.

I wish that I could communicate completely and fully
how real and live this sense of worth and value was to me
as I sat in that moment. There was nothing but me and
the one who created me in His image. I marveled at the
freedom that this granted me and how crucial it was to
everything around me. It meant that everything had to
change. In many ways, it meant for the first time I could
simply embrace being a human. It did not matter if I was
flawed, imperfect, or weak. Nor did it matter if I was
gifted beyond belief with talents, ideas, and avenues of
love. It did not matter if I was mature enough, wise
enough, smart enough, gifted enough, anything enough.
"The things we assume to be ours and give as ours are
borrowed goods, whether it's money, objects, talents,
opportunities, ideas, energies, or even love. We're not
the source….If we try to live independently of the source,
we'll come up empty" (Breton and Largent, *Love, Soul &
Freedom* 82).

It could even be narrowed down to "I am who I am."
This is beautiful because it means embracing not only the
nice parts of myself but the dark parts as well. It means
fully admitting without shame that I don't have life
together nor will I ever. I know certain parts of it but not
all of it and this is okay. I can never know it all so why
should I pretend. Incompleteness is the only reality
within myself that is absolutely certain. This also means
that I can question my gifts, abilities, and talents,
wondering if they truly are my gifts, abilities, and talents,

and if they aren't, what are? It is not a self-doubt but in placing my worth on God, an existence beyond me, there is an invitation to enter further into the reality of who I am. I may not have even discovered my greatest gift amongst what I know of myself. All of this is okay because my importance also does not lie in knowing exactly who I am.

To take it back to me sitting on that brown 70s armchair once more, I may not know what I am even good or bad at because I have never gotten up from that armchair. This is where it became to be a victory for me to destroy the armchair with a hammer and utility knife. I could not, cannot, and am meant and created not to, simply remain on that chair despite the fact that I have an inherent worth and value regardless. The fact that I have an inherent value is great but ultimately it is wasted if I don't share it.

This is where relationship enters. In order to step close and closer to someone, I need a sense of worth and value that gives me the courage and strength to vulnerably stand metaphorically naked in front of another, being who I am at my core, a broken and weak human in need of love and acceptance. A strong sense of worth becomes crucial because it invites humility, honesty, and vulnerability. For example, to accept a friend's feedback can be hard because it can attack our ego. Too often we can get hung up on protecting ourselves, defending ourselves because we fear that someone may see what we fear ourselves, that we are flawed and broken. News flash, we are flawed and broken, get over yourself.

I have -shared this piece of my journey, the importance of sitting at home alone and lonely in a brown 70s armchair, because it has been pivotal in shaping how I view and am attempting to do relationship. In the next few chapters, understanding how I come to process self-worth and identity is essential. In a sense, everything that I have written in this book thus far has been leading to this moment and beyond because, in light of it all, relationships become an invitation into an unfathomable reality of discovery and mystery.

15

The Space Between

I was once asked the question by a wise friend, "What is the space between you and your friends?" While the question was probably asking something about fusion in relationship, fusion referring to a relationship that is so close that individual identities are often lost, my abstract mind immediately jumped to a picture of some sort of metaphysical space that could not be touched, seen, nor heard but clearly existed. And I suppose that it is not rocket science that some sort of space exists between two people in a relationship simply because there are two people involved. Regardless, I became quite intrigued with the idea of a metaphysical space. I began to imagine what it might look like and what it would consist of. As I let my abstract mind run free, I realized that what I was imagining was quickly becoming a conceptualization of relationship. Let me tell you about it.

I see a greyish blue bubble that floats like a cloud in the sky, shimmering and shining magnificently like rays of sun hitting small ripples on a peaceful lake. And similar to the changing and melding colors of a sunset, it can change from a deep, fiery red to the greyish blue that I already suggested, to a brilliant and magnifying yellow. Like a mood ring, it changes based on emotion. And while I call it a bubble, it is unlikely anything you would picture a bubble to be as it is a rough and imperfect changing shape, constantly shrinking and expanding. Did I tell you that it's beautiful? It is probably one of the most beautiful things a person can imagine. Contact with it can bring a smile and has the power to change hearts, becoming a warm hug that embraces, reaching to the deepest recesses of a person's soul. On the opposite end of this spectrum is its ability, with its rough and imperfect exterior, to challenge, grind, and polish the most hardened and calloused parts of a heart.

However, this bubble is also dangerously risky because despite its breathtaking beauty and wonder, it also has the ability to inflict some of the worst kind of pains and hurts. It has the ability to come down in a dark, heavy, and cloudy manifestation that blackens even the brightest of joys. It can cripple and devastate the soul, leaving a life questioning emptiness. It can linger like a black rain cloud that follows a dismal cartoon character. Sometimes it can be a black plague that reeks of death and rotting corpses, frustrating, enraging, and embittering the best of us. Yet, while it has the horrible ability to do what I just described, it does not have to be rotting corpses and pain, and I will get to this.

So, this is the space between, my abstract and conceptualized version of relationship. I just read what I wrote and it really is quite abstract. I wish it were possible to take a picture of what I see in my mind. They say a picture is worth a thousand words. I have used approximately 275 of these words, which means I still have approximately 725 to fully illustrate my abstraction. I surmise that I will need every single one of them, if not more. However, it is not so important that you understand this abstraction as much as it is that I illustrate to you the many things I have learned from looking at this metaphysical space between. I need to focus this illustration by narrowing it down to more concretions. (Yes, this is a word. I surprised myself).

Who owns it?

First of all, I would like to talk about the fact that this space between is not an empty space, it is a metaphysical reality called a relationship. However, since it is metaphysical, without material form, it's something that cannot be tangibly grasped. This would mean that it is beyond human ability to lay ownership to it. No one owns it. Our relationship is not yours and it is not mine. If anything, we share it but I like to think about it as something beyond you or I. It is something that neither you or I could ever fully see or understand, let alone grasp and hold. It is beyond both of us because it is a contribution of thoughts, ideas, feelings, and beliefs. It is a place filled with shared memories, a place of common ground and even uncommon ground. It is a place where the stories that you and I share, and every little piece that we offer of ourselves resides. It is not only a place but also a story of two people, chronicling the journey of a friendship, one that neither you nor I could ever tell. Most importantly however, it is my only connection to you.

Now, since you and I cannot own it, there is no such thing as possessiveness. This is very freeing if you think about it because it can never be stolen. There is a security in knowing that whatever you offered and contributed to the friendship remains and you can never take it back. You can neglect and abandon putting more into the friendship, which I will talk about in the next chapter, but in a sense a card laid is a card played. In fact, if you choose to completely shut yourself off from me, the floating bubble will always remain and it will always be an accessible source of the goodness that it is/was. In fact, this is how I explain how two good friends that have parted ways have the ability to pick up where they left off when they reunite.

Another aspect of this lack of possessiveness is that just because I have some sort of access to you through the space between us that we share, there is no way that I can ever lay claim to who you are. More importantly, to me anyway, you can never lay claim to who I am. The only way I know you is through the space between, and what the space between offers me about you is what you put into the middle yourself, things like body language and any other unspoken communicators that you put forth. There is no way to know the complete version of you. This reality frees me to be me and you to be you, and we will forever be invited into an ever escaping and inviting mystery to discover the other.

I need to point out one more thing about possessiveness. You are not the relationship. I am not the relationship. If the relationship is in a despicable mess and it seems that the bad outweighs the good, oh well. By oh well, I do not necessarily mean lack of care but more of an oh well, shit happens. If the relationship, the space between, cannot be laid claim to, that is to say it is beyond both of us, making no distinct statement about who we are as separate individuals. Therefore, neither of us can take the fact that our relationship is in trouble as something personal. And, in those despicable moments that relationship can be, it comes down to a choice between whether or not it is worth making sense of the space between based on the perceived value that the space between has for each individual. The unfortunate reality, however, is that our minds have the ability to forget how great things are or can be when we are stuck in the middle of shit. I think this is the same reason that suicide can seem like a good option for those in a severely sad state of mind. But never should it be a statement of attack, or about the worth or value of the other person because, as I said earlier, we cannot lay claim to who the other person is. For all we know, he could be hidden behind a wall of fear and doubt that he can't even see. And the wonderful thing about that last statement is that the "for all we know" means that we could speculate until the cows come home and never know. I can never lay claim to knowing who another is or what they are about in any conclusiveness.

The Shimmering and Shining

The shimmering and shining of the space between works much like a mirror. In developing a relationship with someone, something quite magical happens. As we mutually create the space between, I begin to see pieces of you and you of me. "I have my identity and you have yours. I must be myself and you must be yourself. We are called to grow together, each one becoming more fully himself or herself" (Vanier, *From Brokenness to Community* 17). Some of what I put into the space between will be things I am quite aware of, and likewise. However, there are other things, like my body language, my tone of voice, or repeated behaviors or actions that I may not be aware of. This is where the shimmering and shining like sun rays on ripples of a lake come in. The space between becomes like a mirror in which I can learn more about myself.

This mirror, a reflection of myself, is made out of two things. Most blatantly is what the other person tells me through the space between, making observations and statements about who I appear to be. Take, for example, someone calling me a complainer. The only way the other person would see this is through the space between. However, similar to the distortion that ripples cause in a reflection on a lake, it is impossible, as I mentioned in the last section, for the statements of the other to be absolutely certain. The only way my friend's image of me, as complainer, can become real in all certainty is if I choose to truly and honestly look at the reflection of myself that is offered. This might mean looking at other reflections of me offered from the space between other people but, ultimately, it comes down to truly considering the parts of myself that get reflected back.

In order to do this, a great amount of humility is needed because sometimes the image that gets reflected in the space between is far from beautiful. The beautiful thing about the space between is that eventually it becomes inevitable that not only the good parts of ourselves will be put into the space between but also the weak and vulnerable parts, the ones that need to be reflected and loved. We can only hold a façade for so long before the real parts of ourselves, the parts we like to keep hidden, begin to be exposed in the smallest of our actions. Our tone of voice may be a clue, added to another clue contained in small and seemingly insignificant statement. I simply need to humbly and graciously accept that I do not have it together and what is offered in a reflection could very well be true.

I learned much in taking seriously the claims that friends make of me and have been shocked at times with some of my friends' abilities to pin-point some of my greatest fears, pains, struggles, or make statements about me that I thought no one but I knew. It can be painfully vulnerable to experience this and sometimes I have caught myself distancing myself from people out of protection, even giving up on friendships that seemed to be able to see right through me. This can be painful but it can also be the greatest opportunity to receive the love and acceptance that those painful parts that have been exposed need. Ultimately, I want to be the best me that I can be. This means allowing the reflections of the space between to be considered. Just as it is impossible to see my face without a mirror, I sometimes don't know that I have spinach in my teeth. I need to trust the spaces in between in my life to let me know about the spinach in my teeth. At the same time, I need to give the space between grace enough to be wrong. Maybe it is not spinach in my teeth but a piece of green goop sitting on the lens of their glasses.

And this leads me to my second point about what a reflection in the space between is made out of. Sometimes, just like the green goop on the lens of their glasses, we have the ability to reflect through the space between something that is about us, not the other. I could easily say to you, "Man oh man, you come off as too perfect." And quite possibly you could be too polished and standoffish because of it. Another option is that I could be reflecting a false image of yourself back to you out of my own imperfection. It could be that, without even being aware, I am so scared of feeling inferior and of being rejected that I make an immediate defense against your seeming confidence. My statement about you being too perfect would be more a statement about my lack of confidence than it would be about you being perfect.

The only way you or I am allowed to speak into the space between is if we both allow each other to be completely and utterly wrong. My perceptions of reality get mixed in the space between with your perceptions of reality, making no room for an absolute reality. The space between becomes a beautiful mystery that we are invited into, one that will change us forever as we let our reflections shine and bring brilliance. There can be no such thing as unrealistic expectations because whatever we put into the space between has the opportunity to mix and mingle with the thoughts of the other. Instead, what plays out is that if I seemingly express expectations of you and we let them mingle in the air with your thoughts, what will become clear is my need and weakness inviting love and acceptance, and your ability, willingness and capacity to love and accept. It invites further depth but it never demands it. It seeks to understand the space between and discover the unknown potential. So, it is never about demanding expectation, it is about determining the nameless and boundless possibilities that the space between is and can be.

One more noteworthy point about the shimmering and shining reflections that the space between offers needs to be clarified. Relationship opens up the opportunity to not only know another but also ourselves. I would argue that it is impossible to know yourself in a more full and complete way without the space between. "We do not discover who we are, we do not reach true humanness, in a solitary state; we discover it through mutual dependency, in weakness, in learning through belonging" (Vanier, *Becoming Human* 41). As I engage with the space between, watching perceptions of reality mingle, I learn that I am both similar and greatly different than my friend. With a space between, I can watch from a distance the life of a friend, both learning from him and further defining who I am. I learn a part of who I am in experiencing the similarities and the differences that are shared in the space between. It becomes about absolute respect and honor for the differences because they challenge, inspire, and even complement the other. Similarities become the joy and happiness that keep us connected as fellow humans.

The Sad Spaces Between

Sometimes, the space between can be rotting corpses and pain. I don't like when this happens. This greatly reflects back to the chapter called "Rules of Engagement and Stumbling Drunks." My heart really grieves when I see the spaces between around me, in my own life and in others, reeking of rotting corpses and pain when I know how great relationships are. On top of which we are all so valuable and important, all worthy of respect and dignity, all having something to offer another, and yet somehow we end up neglecting the space between. We push others away, avoiding the great potential that a good space between has. And while no one can lay claim to owning the space between, both you and I maintain it. If I begin to neglect maintenance, it is unfair to you because it leaves you hanging. I have two options to avoid rotting corpses and limit the pain. I can either communicate care and concern and step into maintaining, or I can offer the respect and dignity of ending the space between properly by acknowledging what the space is and was, instead of walking away as if it never existed.

There is also sadness because there is a very subjective nature to spaces between. What I see, the beauty, the potential, the love, the respect, and the dignity, could be dreadfully horrible, scary, or unknown to you. Beauty is the eye of the beholder. This is why I think it is important to make an effort to see the beauty that others see, having a dialogue about the space between that we share. This allows for the beautiful things to become even more beautiful, strengthening the space between. It can also bring forth the ugly. However, I am convinced that the ugly can only grow bigger if we do not acknowledge the fact that there is another person just like us, needing the same love and acceptance that we need on the other side of the gap known as the space between. And the dignity and respect that this inquires should sadly never lead to rotten corpses and pain. If anything, it should provide the opportunity for an even better understanding of the space between, inviting depth and understanding.

16

I Have a Confession About Birds

Along while back when I was younger and more naïve than I am now, well, the younger part is at least true, I came across a letter addressed to one of my roommates from his ex-girlfriend. I still feel guilty saying this, despite the fact that it was probably over ten years ago now, but I read the letter. While I am not proud of this moment, I am confessing it now. I also need to tell you about the bird part because that letter got me thinking about and processing this current chapter. My roommate's ex-girlfriend's sentimental letter included something about a bird combined with the old adage that states, "If you love something, set it free and if it comes back, it's yours. If it doesn't, it never was yours." My mind has gone to town over the years processing and developing the imagery that was contained in that letter. Before I go any further, I need to change the old adage because I despise its possessive language. This is what I think it should say, "If you love something, set it free and if it comes back, be grateful. If it doesn't, be grateful." This begs of divulgence.

The whole point of talking about this confession about birds is to illustrate, in addition to the space between way of looking at relationships, I also look at them in relation to birds. We are all birds, created to spread our wings and fly. The weakest and most vulnerable among us are gifted and talented beyond our mind's knowledge. Jean Vanier talks about one aspect of love being revelation. He writes, "To reveal someone's beauty is to reveal their value by giving them time, attention, and tenderness. To love is not just to do something for them but to reveal to them their uniqueness, to tell them that they are special and worthy of attention" (*Becoming Human* 22). To help someone become who they are meant to be, to help them discover their gifts, encouraging them, speaking through weakness and brokenness, is one of, if not the most important, aspect of friendship. Friendship becomes a place where we mutually discover our wings to fly and begin to soar, inviting the opportunity for others to join us. Together, we can collectively soar to heights beyond our wildest imaginations.

How this exactly happens is encapsulated in the morphing ability we have as birds to change into strong, firmly grounded statues. We are also like great big statues, similar to something like *Christ the Redeemer* that overlooks Rio de Janeiro, with arms invitingly open wide. In our wide-open arms, we invite relationship, birds, to come rest upon our open arms, just like you see birds stopping to rest on statues.

There are a great many advantages in reminding myself of this illustration. First of which is that a statue is still a statue without any birds resting on it. I am created for relationship and to be in relationship but if I have any birds currently resting upon me or not says nothing about my stature as a statue. I am firmly and concretely established on the things that I learned about my inherent worth from sitting on a brown 70s armchair. I do not need to worry or keep a tally of the birds that choose to rest and visit.

However, sometimes I forget that I am a statue with arms and hands invitingly open and think that my arms and hands are closed. When I think this, I have a tendency to wait until a bird comes near and then quickly open my hands to grasp it. And once it's grasped, I hold it near and dear, smothering it, crippling the bird's ability to fly. I need to be vulnerable enough to leave my arms and hands open to invite, as they truly are. If I am being true to myself, trusting the worth and value inherent in me, I know that I have something really great to offer those birds that choose to rest in my hand. It is up to them to come sit, rest and be loved, held and cherished.

And statues can't move. As a statue, I need to trust that the birds, the relationships, that I am meant and created to have, will come to me as I have my arms extended in invitation. I cannot reach or grasp. I learn to fully be who I am, letting the birds come. And part of this being who I am involves the weak and vulnerable parts of myself as well because

> the more we cry out from our souls – cry out that we don't know what to do with our lives, cry out that we don't know how to help someone we love

who's in pain, cry out that we don't know what's
happening to our planet, cry out that we don't
know where to begin to help ourselves and our
world – the more profoundly we experience our
need, and the more help comes our way. (Breton
and Largent, *Love, Soul & Freedom* 96-7)

The birds will come and when they do, I also have the
ability to morph back to the bird I am and allow myself to
rest on the statue that others are. It is almost as if the
bird and the statue exist in one. We have the ability to fly
and rest, and we have the ability to provide rest for
others. Relationships viewed in this way become a
beautiful expression of freely offering and freely
receiving. It does not ask or demand, and there is a free
flow of love and it begs that I trust the things I need will
come to me. Hence the freedom to say, "If you love
something, set it free and if it comes back, be grateful. If
it doesn't, be grateful."

Possessive jealousy, manipulation, control, and the
competition to be the best friend I can be becomes
absolutely impossible in light of a thought line like this. I
need to let relationship, the birds that come, bring life
and love to me, being fully aware that there is nothing I
can do to keep them from flying away, and nothing apart
from being who I am in all my weakness and strength that
can hold them captive. This can be terribly scary because
it asks complete and utter trust from those birds around
us and can make us appear to be less secure. The reality
is that I need to trust that there will be birds that learn to
see the true beauty and value of who I am, and, once they
have, they will choose to stay. Ultimately, there is more
security in this because I will know that those birds that
choose to continue to sit and rest are not there because

of something I did but because of who I am. I will have security in the fact that they are there with me because they want to be and I will never have to doubt that they may be there because I am possessive, manipulative, or competing for their friendship.

This may mean the admission that I may, as a bird, get more out of sitting on the hand of another than that same friend, or bird, may enjoy resting on my hand. This could mean that I have not opened my hands enough, inviting them closer. It could also mean that they have refused to allow themselves to truly rest and see the beauty that I am. It is important that we take note of these moments and challenge ourselves, with the mirror effects of the space between. I need to learn to open up. Something that I have not gone as much into depth about is that I also need to allow myself to land and rest on the open and inviting arms of another. This is not always easy because it involves expressing the vulnerability of need. I think to often I sneakily land and rest without letting the statue know. I will land, seeking rest and refuge in my friend, asking for love and acceptance but refusing to let them know what I need, placing unknown and false expectations upon them. And then when they do not notice I am there, I am hurt that they did not acknowledge me.

In the end it comes down to the fact that "[f]riendship and love cannot develop in the form of an anxious clinging to each other. They ask for gentle fearless space in which we can move to and from each other." (Nouwen 30). It allows the space between, having our hands open without grasping, inviting others to be who they are as together we discover our wings to fly.

17

The Divine

I have yet to talk about my most important relationship. I have not wanted to. In fact, I almost decided that I would not even talk about it. I have come to the conclusion that it is near impossible to talk, or write, around something so important and valuable to me. My intent in trying to avoid direct discussion about this relationship is not to avoid communicating about it but to protect it from what it is not. It is my relationship with the Divine that I speak of: My relationship with Jesus, the fact that I have Jesus in my heart. So clichéd are these phrases that I greatly fear the meaning, my real and living connection to the Divine, will be lost in communication.

As I wrote the introduction to this book, I had my very dear friend Tim read it. One of his critiques, and rightfully so, was "What's with talking about God as the

'Divine'? He does have a name!" Tim knew better than I that there was a part of me shying away from what my Dad once encouraged me to do in my writing, "You tell it how it is!" I fear calling Jesus by name, or making statements about a relationship with Him, because it seems, at times, that the notions and concepts that people have when I do talk about Jesus are not close to the notions and concepts that I have. I fear that the name Jesus has become cliché and has become distant from the real Jesus that I claim to know and have a relationship with. And so, in protection of the Jesus I know and love, I decided to start out by calling Him the Divine.

I sense the rolling of eyes and the scoffing of some who may be reading this. I do not blame you because within the terminology that I have used there is an, "Ugh... Christians... ugh...Jesus talk... here we go, Evangelical Christianity!" I know this to be true because this is my reaction to some of the words, terminology, phraseology, beliefs, and opinions that get thrown around in regards to Jesus, God, and Christianity. Here is an example that makes me laugh and sigh sadly every time I think about it. I know this wonderful woman who is a genuine seeker of truth but, like all of us, has the ability to get seemingly lost in her own delirium. She was telling a group of us a story about a squirrel. In the story, she told us that she had her ground-level and screenless window open, and how she had noticed there were some squirrels running around outside. Long story short, she said, "It was the Lord's timing that I looked up just in time to be able to close the window before a squirrel ran into my room." My instant and internal reaction was "Really? ... sigh ... really ... the Lord's timing?" and then my external reaction delivered in a joking tone, "Or maybe it was not the Lord's timing and you were meant to have a visitor in

your room, like Balaam's donkey." This Biblical donkey
was enabled to talk to his owner, Balaam, for a brief
moment.

I give this example because I know and have
experienced the sometimes sickening and revolting
nature of the evangelical Christianity that I supposedly lay
claim to. I fear, or maybe hate, claiming to even be a
Christian at times because the concepts that people have
about what or who a Christian is often has nothing to do
with who I am nor anything to do with Christ Himself.

You should presume that from the way I am talking
that there is nothing that I do that shies away from who
Christ truly is. You would be certainly correct in
presuming such a wonderful statement if it weren't for
just this one time. I once shamefully initiated a
conversation, or possibly an interrogation, with a woman
about her opinion on me going to a Christian University in
hopes that I could tell her about how she needs Christ. I
cringe to this day. Oh, and there was this one other time
when I lent a girl I worked with a Bible and I told her to
read portions of it, as if I were an authoritative teacher
giving homework. I even checked up on her assignment
the next day. I think I just puked in my mouth. It was just
these two times though. Sarcasm aside, it was these two
times and probably a million other times since. I want to
live as truthful to Christ and what He represents but I
would be both a liar and a hypocrite to say that I
represent Him and who He is to the fullest, or maybe
even slightest. I am truly sorry. I am sorry to the woman I
once interrogated and I am sorry to the girl I worked with
that I horribly Bible-thumped. I am also sorry to everyone
reading this who has endured or experienced this
revolting and disgusting type of Christianity. I am

shamefully embarrassed of how the faith I claim stake in has drug itself through the dirt time and again and then calls the world's reaction persecution. We of the faith, myself included, have represented Christ inaccurately at times, maybe most times, and I am sad because Christ is not who many think He is nor does He represent much of what people think He does. Again, I am sorry.

I can never promise that something I say or do, or write for that matter, as a Christian won't leave a puke taste in your mouth. If that is or has been the case, and I apologize if it is, I am almost certain it has no bearing on who Jesus really is and that I have misrepresented Him. This I know. Interaction with the real Jesus can be uncomfortable, stretching, challenging, and even painful but He is not grotesquely sickening, weak, inauthentic, fake, forcefully in your face, or annoying.

So, this is what I will ask of my reader, maybe even plead, as I write this last section. Please grant me the grace to be honest and vulnerable with the most important relationship I have: The Jesus in my heart relationship. At the same time, I ask that you would not be quick to judge who Jesus is and based on what I write in regards to having a relationship with Him. I could know you quite well and I could know much about your life. I may even get to know much about your closest friend as you talk about him/her. I may even grow to like your friend based on what you say. On the other hand, I may grow to hate them based on what you say. But, at the end of the day, I cannot claim to know who your friend is and what they stand for, based on what you say about them. Please don't judge your opinion of Jesus, and the truth of who He is, on what I may say. Ultimately, I guess my fear is that I do not want to drag the name of Jesus through the mud anymore than it has already been dragged. However, based on the fact that I am a human with a limited mind that happens to be tainted with, and by, the broken world around me, it is impossible for me to clearly represent the truth as I talk about Jesus, or any topic for that matter. I will not and cannot protect Jesus, and I refuse to. Jesus can stand up for Himself. All I can do, and will do, is be as honest, open, and vulnerable about my experience of the Divine in relationship as my heart will allow.

In my attempt to protect Jesus, I realize and will admit that I am also attempting to protect myself. My occasional embarrassment with the Christianity around me aside, I don't want to look or sound like a weird and strange person living in a hallucinatory world with an imaginary friend whose name is Jesus. To say that my closest friend came down to earth as a baby born out of a virgin womb, died on a cross, came back to life and now lives in my heart seems absolutely ridiculous if a person thinks rationally about it. And I do rationally think about it from time to time and it has, and does, lead me to moments where I question the sanity of my beliefs. Counterintuitive to this question of sanity is some sort of strange faith, knowledge, or connection that I do not know how to explain exactly but anchors me to these obscure and strange beliefs.

I want you to know I am not crazy, stupid, or weak for having these crazy beliefs and part of me wants prove it. The other part of me wants to hide and protect myself so you don't see how crazy I may appear on the surface. Instead, I invite you into my Jesus in my heart relationship. In wanting to prove and protect Jesus, and myself, authenticity, honesty, and vulnerability will be my only defense. I am going to refuse to come off as trying to prove anything and I also refuse to come off as trying to protect Jesus and the connection I have to him. This means that I am simply going to tell it how it is for me. Doubt will be doubt and frustration will be frustration. I can only say what my experience has told me and I will tell as much as my heart will allow. And this is where you are invited, into the honesty and openness of one person's connection to the Divine. It is what it is.

You may wonder why I would bother writing or reflecting on a topic that I apprehensively had to write a massive disclaimer on. To answer this, I would like to quote a 13th century Sufi mystic, "There is no reality but God. There is only God" (qtd. in Breton and Largent, *Love, Soul & Freedom* 82). God is where this whole discussion of friendship, relationship, resides. It starts and ends with God. I feel it becomes absolutely impossible to leave the lengthy discussion of this book without an explicit statement.

The Bible says that love comes from God and that God is love. This opens up a whole new way of thinking about Bob Marley's "One Love". If all Love is God, every relationship that contains love also contains a taste of God. The love I give my friends, and the love I receive from my friends tells of goodness and the greatness of the only true, pure and perfect love, called God. This connects me to an unfathomable reality because every relationship, every person, becomes an avenue in discovering a piece of God. I can no longer be connected to others without, at some point, acknowledging what it says about God, true love. Mother Teresa said, "The dying, the cripple, the mental, the unwanted, the unloved-- they are Jesus in disguise" (Desmond n.p.) She found God in the people that societies often label as the weakest and having the least to offer.

The Bible also says that man was created in the image of God. This means whether I choose to or not there is something about who I am as a human that conveys God. If God is love, then I am created in the image of love. This means that everyone around me, whoever they are and create themselves to be, regardless of religion or beliefs, communicates to me something about God. Relationship becomes the avenue to discovering an image of God, a reflection of the one and only love. Everyone I communicate with becomes a vessel containing the true source and reflection of love.

I have decided that we all can be like the Biblical prophet Hosea if we want to. God told Hosea to marry a prostitute. This may seem like a strange request but what happened to Hosea in his experience of being married to an unfaithful woman became an analogy of the relationship between God and His people in Israel. While I am sure that we could find a prostitute to marry, this is not what I mean. Like Hosea we can look at our relationships as analogies of the relationship that God has with us.

Human relationship is tangible, making it arguably one of the best ways that relationship with God can be made real and life giving. I have learned from the time I was a baby how to interact with others and I have developed all sorts of relational dynamics and ways of interrelating, many of which are not the healthiest or most wholesome. All I know relationship to be is based upon the tangible interactions of people around me. If I allow my relationships to become analogies of a relationship with God, I am ushered into an opportunity to be opened up to God. Essentially, every relational problem I have with people turns out to be the same relational problems that keep me distant from God. If I am too proud, arrogant, and ignorant, having learned to be self-sufficient, and I notice that I do not let people take care of me and truly let them into my life, I have to be honest enough to admit that I probably also put this onto God as well, or who or what I believe God to be. It comes down to striving for all the things I talked about in this book and then some. If we open ourselves to fully living our relationships, we can't help but be confronted with a higher reality.

It goes further than this. I want to jump back to the thought of God being love and then combine it with this idea of us being prophets. If God is love, the love I offer to my friends contains a taste of God. This means that the love I feel, from the butterflies in my stomach to that gut wrenching pain I get when I see a friend struggling and I know there is nothing I can do about it, is the same love that God has for me. How I appreciate my friend is how God appreciates me. All the love I have for my friends is the all the love that God has for me but all the more because God does it in perfection.

On the other side of this is how hurt and pain in relationship speaks of God as well. I have already expressed a few times, I think, my detest and frustration with broken relationships. In these situations, at some point it always comes down to completely missing the other; a misunderstanding, needs were neglected or not communicated. In disagreement and broken relationships, I would argue that it always comes down to both parties saying, "They have no idea." The sad part is that at times we have done everything we know how to do in order to meet eye to eye, and time and time again our hurt and brokenness yet again collides with the other's hurt and brokenness. I have been left in the broken places of relationship, remaining with an open hand of vulnerability, saying to myself, "Can't you see that I am just doing my best to love you in the best way I know how?" This statement brings me more pain because attempting to love while standing in the face of rejection takes all the strength I have. I may have done all I can, all I know how to do, and still I am left standing there as if I were the weak one for letting myself be vulnerable.

And then I am drawn to Jesus facing the rejection he faced. I cannot imagine what it would feel like to know that you were going to die for all of humanity, your life as a sacrifice, and then for humanity to crucify you. Sacrificing your life for those who are rejecting you by nailing you to a cross does not sound pleasant. One of Jesus' reactions in this moment, as I mentioned previous, was the prayer "Father, forgive them, for they know not what they do." I can almost hear him saying "If only they knew or understood how much I actually love them." I can't help but think about this when I think back to the times when all I have attempted to do was love the best way I knew how and was seemingly rejected for it, all the times that I attempted to reach out and was rejected.

This feeling of rejection, this wretched pain, illuminates the love God has for me. I have loved some people a lot and in some cases have been met with rejection with no explanation why. And then I realize I do this all the time. I reject God when all He is attempting to do is be who He is... Love. I find myself pushing away out of fear of who He is. I am scared of perfect love. Perfect love asks for vulnerability, humility, truth and there is little room to hide. This is ironic because the bible says that "[t]here is no fear in love. But perfect love drives out fear, because fear has to do with punishment. The one who fears is not made perfect in love" (1 John 4:18). Although I suppose, what am I hiding from? Hiding speaks of shame and guilt, which can metaphorically be a place of punishment. I started talking about feeling rejected in a relationship and I am left with the realization that I hide myself from God. I actually didn't intend this and I am quite somber as I write at this moment because I know I have some prayer and reflection to do.

I got to this place in reflecting on the relationships in my life. They have become priceless tools of invitation to know God. People, relationships, connect me with God. This has become somewhat cyclic to me because it seems that the more I enter into the concept of God, and relate with the person of God, the more I am drawn to connect with the people around me. And the more I connect with the people around me, the more I am drawn back to God.

Relationship is the discovery of love and Love is God. A good relationship is a beckoning into the arms of my creator. It can be the scariest thing ever because sometimes it can be so unreal that I conclude that it must be a hoax, does not exist and is not real, and then chalk it up to whatever excuse I can make. True love can be cutting, harsh, and inviting of change, and sometimes I am too scared to change. God is perfect at it and I try my best. And that is greatly what this book is about, my attempt at love. It is a beautiful thing to attempt because in the process I not only find myself in the deepest appreciation of those around me but also within the embrace of Perfect Love, God.

18

Conclusion

This is the chapter in which we part ways. This somewhat scares me because this is the last chapter that I am writing, which means that this book is one step closer to being published and in the hands of you, the reader. I am scared of this, to be honest, because I am worried that I will be missed, misunderstood, or rejected in a great many things I have been vulnerable about. My hope is that you have found yourself somewhere along the way. I have challenged myself to be as honest and as open as I could because my greatest commonality with you is our brokenness as humans. I thought it was a good meeting point.

Another fear is that I am going to come off as being arrogant, self-righteous, or ignorant, or a combination of all three. About two weeks back I was talking with my Uncle about me writing a book. He laughed and asked,

"What do you know? You see those people out there writing about one thing and then a year later writing the exact opposite thing." This made me laugh and I responded with, "No-one knows anything." I have decided that the minute I let myself think that I do know something will be the exact same minute that I give up truly searching and seeking out pure incorruptible truth.

I am on a life-long journey of perfecting and fine tuning life and relationships. For as long as I remain imperfect, there will always be more that I can learn and embrace about relationships. I am quite passionate about friendships, if that has not become evident quite yet. Often I am struck by a deep, hurting sadness, wanting so much for the people around me. I don't think we realize the potential that our friendships or our relationships have. We have the greatest opportunity to become all that we were meant to be if we open ourselves up. As we come together in our common humanity, in all our hurt, brokenness, and weakness, there is an unbelievable and beautiful reality waiting for us.

Sometimes this is hard because culture and society often dictate how relationships work, and how they play out. I get stuck trying to challenge the norm and it becomes difficult because I can catch people off guard. In catching people off guard, I can appear immature, unrealistic, judgmental, analytical, and plain old annoying. Not to long ago I was told, "I think you don't know how to do relationship because you are a counsellor and you just point out peoples' flaws." I felt completely misunderstood and this pained me greatly because I love people a lot. I suppose there is much I could unpack in regards to pointing out flaws but I am leaving this statement as it is. Neither I nor the person who gave me that comment has yet to perfect love.

Another thing against me is my maleness. I think all of us males have a bit of an uphill battle when it comes to making true connections with other guys. I was struck with a frustrating grief one day when I went into a pub washroom and above the urinal found an advertisement about wings that stated, "Men share wings not feelings." Men are to be strong and confident because boys don't cry. *The Secrets Men Keep*, by Ken Druck with James C. Simmons discusses one of the only socially acceptable ways that guys can truly share the deeper parts of themselves is over a beer; "Short of having sex together, two men may do just about anything as long as there is beer present" (96). If this is true, based on my desire for good friendship, I may need to become an alcoholic. I think something needs to give. I can't help but wonder how much I have written in this book is a statement regarding men and how men do friendship.

I think that it is hard to find good friendships. It is one thing to find people that you can spend time with but truly sharing life with others is a completely different thing. It is my experience that true and good friends are few and far between. I try to hold onto it when I do find it, and I will fight tooth and nail for it, even if I look like an absolute idiot. Everything within this book seeks and speaks to that.

Mother Teresa said, "I have found the paradox that if I love until it hurts, then there is no hurt but only more love"(qtd. in Mother Teresa of Calcutta Quotes n.p.). Truly opening oneself to love is one of the most painful and beautiful things a person can do. There is an incredible and profound reality to be discovered, one that connects me more fully to who I am meant to be and invites me into Perfect Love, God. It extends to the greatest depths and the highest heights, expanding beyond me, into the people and the world around me.

And maybe everything I have written is simply too idealistic. Maybe I am living in a dream world. The vivid dream that I had and started this book with initiated the whole dialogue that this book has become. Then again, I think sometimes, maybe most times, we are called to live in the pain of unrealistic ideals of love and relationship for the benefit of those around us in hopes of restoring the human heart and world to its unbroken state. And while sometimes, maybe most times, I can't do this; I have heard that we only have ability to change one heart at a time. I do have the ability to be a friend and so do you.

Also, Please read the thank-yous at the end of this book

Works Cited

Bentall, Barney. "Oh Shelly." *Barney Bentall: Greatest Hits 1986-1996*. Golden Cage Music Ltd., 1996.

Bloomfield, Harold H. *Making Peace With Your Parents*. Random House Inc., 1983

Breton, Denise, and Christopher Largent. *Love, Soul & Freedom: Dancing with Rumi on the Mystic Path*. Center City, Minnesota: Hazeldon, 1998.

Breton, Denise, and Christopher Largent. *The Paradigm Conspiracy: Why Our Social Systems Violate Human Potential – And How We Can Change Them*. Center City, Minnesota: Hazeldon, 1996.

Cacioppo, John T., and William Patrick. *Loneliness: Human Nature and the Need for Social Connection.* New York: W.W. Norton and Company, 2008.

Dali, Salvador, and Andre Parinaud. *Maniac Eyeball: The Unspeakable Confessions Of Salvador Dali.* Solar Books, 2008.

Desmond, Edward W. "Interview with MOTHER Teresa: A Pencil In the Hand Of God - TIME." *Breaking News, Analysis, Politics, Blogs, News Photos, Video, Tech Reviews - TIME.com*. Web. 20 June 2011. <http://www.time.com/time/magazine/article/0,91 71,959149,00.html>.

Epstein, Joseph. *Snobbery: The American Version*. New York: Houghton Mifflin Company, 2002.

Everly Brothers. "When Will I Be Loved." *30 Original Hits (Remastered)*. Play Digital, 2011.

Feldman, Robert. *The Liar in Your Life: The Way to Truthful Relationships*. New York: Twelve, 2009.

Fitzgerald, Michael Bernard. "Brand New Spaces." *The MBF Love LP*. Load Music, 2009.

Frankl, Victor E. *Man's Search For Meaning.* Boston: Frey, James. *A Million Little Pieces.* New York: Anchor Books, 2004.

Fromm, Erich. *The Art of Loving*. New York: Harper and Row Publishers, 1989.

Gilbert, Daniel. *Stumbling on Happiness*. New York: Vintage Books, 2005.

McGinnis, Alan Loy. *The Friendship Factor: How to get closer to the people you care for.* Minneapolis: Augsburg Publishing House, 1979.

"Mother Teresa of Calcutta Quotes." *Find the Famous Quotes You Need, ThinkExist.com Quotations.* Web. 20 June 2011. <http://en.thinkexist.com/quotation/i_have_found_t he_paradox_that_if_i_love_until_it/14300.html>.

NIV. *The Holy Bible, New International Version.* Grand Rapids, Michigan: Zondervan, 2006.

Nouwen, Henri J.M.. *Reaching Out: The Three Movements of the Spiritual Life*. New York: Doubleday, 1986.

Richardson, Ronald W. *Creating a Healthier Church*. Minneapolis, MN: Fortress Press, 1996.

Rufus, Anneli. *Party of One: The Loner's Manifesto*. New York: Marlowe & Company, 2003.

Salinger, J.D.. *The Catcher in the Rye*. Boston, MA: Little, Brown and Company, 1951.

Vanier, Jean. *Becoming Human.* Toronto: Anansi Press, 1998.

Vanier, Jean. *From Brokenness to Community.* Mahwah, NJ: Paulist Press, 1992.

Thank-Yous in No Specific Order

To you, my reader. Thanks for journeying along with me.

To all my friends, my family, and all the people I know, for
without permission you have allowed yourselves and the
relationships I have with you to be my ground for
research. You are all in here somewhere. Thanks for all
the conversations and the truths that you have conveyed
to me. A special thanks to those who I have quoted and
used stories about.

To Mike Morelli and the Olive Tree Ochestra for a genuine
and real musical expression of the Perfect Love. It will
forever be tied to writing this book. **Check it out:**
http://www.myspace.com/theolivetreeorchestra

To Mom and Dad for all the support, both now and in the
past. Most recently allowing me to stay for a month, rent
free, so that I could write.

To Baba, who has continually offers her love in any way
she can think of, which often ends up as items of food.
Most recently, however, it was allowing me to stay at her
house and write.

To my siblings who know me better than I think at times.
Thanks for everything.

To a former friend, who chooses to remain as such, who
has challenged me like few others ever have. Also, thanks
man for the green mug that has been a permanent fixture
beside my laptop.

To my great friend Kelly, whose support is arguably matched by few and has provided encouragement like no other.

To Tim, who I have more in common with than I think and challenges me to be more of who I am meant and created to be in the stark differences that we are.

To Ness, who has modeled and challenged me to be the vulnerability that I have wrote about.

To my oldest life-long friend, Sarah. Thanks for appearing in the dream that became the true beginning of this book.

To Cam and Leigh, for your priceless friendship but also for the introduction to this book because it was written on your back patio.

To Pam, for being a great friend and host, and for providing me with a cabin by the ocean to write.

To Jerry and Amy, my family in Calgary, for the priceless friendship that has stood the test of time, and has contributed greatly to my confidence in stepping out and getting this done.

To Lisa, for your thorough editing as well as all of your helpful suggestions.

To Jon, for formatting, and helping with putting it all together. Also, for the very out of the blue friendship!

Also to everyone that I have missed and will have a bone to pick with me later!

8967984R0

Made in the USA
Charleston, SC
30 July 2011